The Bike Deconstructed

The Bike Deconstructed

A Grand Tour of the Road Bicycle

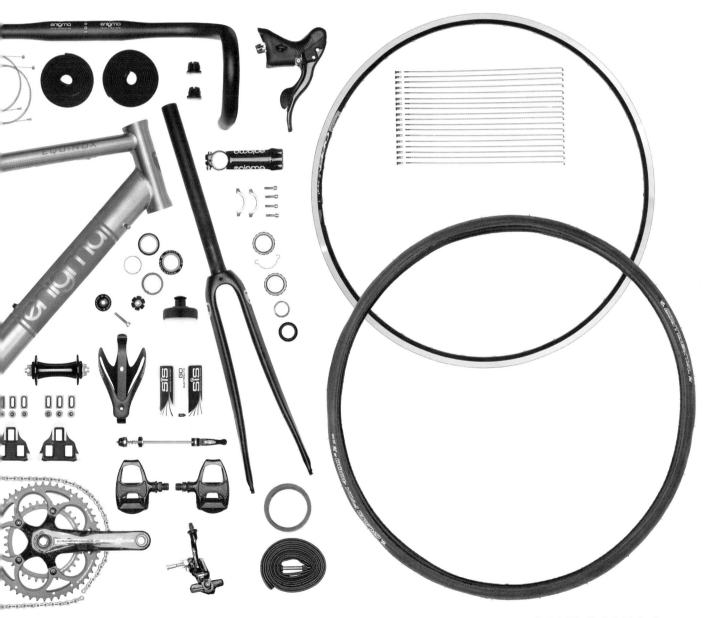

Richard Hallett

MITCHELL
BEAZLEY

For Jan

The Bike Deconstructed
Author: Richard Hallett

First published in Great Britain in 2014 by Mitchell Beazley,
an imprint of Octopus Publishing Group Ltd,
Endeavour House, 189 Shaftesbury Avenue, London WC2H 8JY
www.octopusbooks.co.uk

An Hachette UK Company
www.hachette.co.uk

ISBN: 978 1 84533 883 1

A CIP record of this book is available from the British Library

Set in Plantin MT Pro and Galaxie Polaris

Printed and bound in China

Mitchell Beazley Publisher: Alison Starling

Conceived, designed and produced by
Quid Publishing
Level 4 Sheridan House
Hove BN3 1DD
England

Design: Paul Palmer-Edwards, Grade Design
Technical illustration: Matt Pagett
Copy editor: Simon Smythe

Contents

Foreword   8

Introduction   10

Anatomy of a Bike   12

1

MATERIALS

Materials: Overview   16

Carbon-Fibre   18

Steel   20

Titanium   22

Aluminium   24

2

FRAMESET

Frame Evolution   28

Frameset: Tubes   32

Frameset: Front Fork   42

Headset   46

Suspension   48

3

WHEELS

Wheels: A Short History   52

Wheel Tension   56

Rims: Types   60

Tyres: A Short History   62

Tyres: Construction   66

Tyres: Performance   68

Spokes   70

Nipples   72

Hubs   74

Quick Release   78

Freehub   80

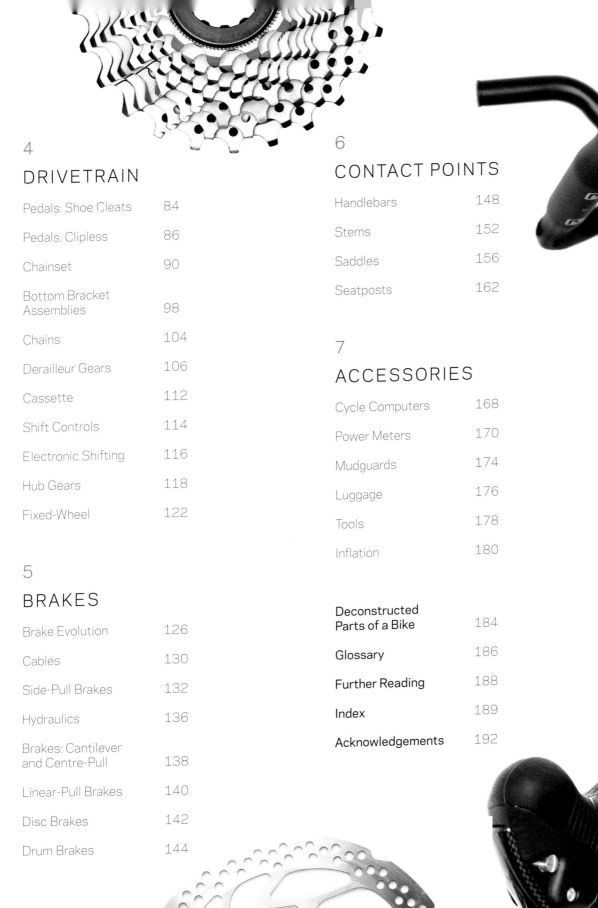

4

DRIVETRAIN

Pedals: Shoe Cleats	84
Pedals: Clipless	86
Chainset	90
Bottom Bracket Assemblies	98
Chains	104
Derailleur Gears	106
Cassette	112
Shift Controls	114
Electronic Shifting	116
Hub Gears	118
Fixed-Wheel	122

5

BRAKES

Brake Evolution	126
Cables	130
Side-Pull Brakes	132
Hydraulics	136
Brakes: Cantilever and Centre-Pull	138
Linear-Pull Brakes	140
Disc Brakes	142
Drum Brakes	144

6

CONTACT POINTS

Handlebars	148
Stems	152
Saddles	156
Seatposts	162

7

ACCESSORIES

Cycle Computers	168
Power Meters	170
Mudguards	174
Luggage	176
Tools	178
Inflation	180

Deconstructed Parts of a Bike	184
Glossary	186
Further Reading	188
Index	189
Acknowledgements	192

Foreword

There can be hardly a soul alive in the modern world who has not at some point in his or her life owned, ridden and enjoyed a bicycle.

It has been a bringer of social and financial emancipation or of personal freedom, a vector for the genetic spread in human populations, a chariot of warring armies and most importantly an invention that satisfies man's ancient desire to travel through the natural world in which he lives.

Over the last decade this simple and satisfying invention has once again gripped the imagination of new riders all around the globe and introduced a whole new generation of men and women to the simple pleasures of the bicycle. To many of these new riders knowledge of the machine and its origins remains uncharted territory.

Reading this book I am reminded that the form and function of the bicycle itself is as elegant and beautiful as the act of riding one. It took me back to long days as a boy stripping and rebuilding my own paper round hacks and transported me into the fascinating engineering that makes up the modern bike.

Knowledge and abiding love of the bicycle are evident on each page and having ridden with the author on many occasions I've never come away from our outings without some new snippet of information.

The Bike Deconstructed is akin to a very long ride with the author – one where your understanding of this most popular and enduring invention is constantly enhanced and, even better, you don't even have to sling your leg over a top tube and ride to enjoy the learning experience!

David Harmon
Professional Sports Commentator

Introduction

If the bicycle is the world's greatest invention, then the road
bike is surely its ultimate incarnation. Not because it is
lighter, faster or more glamorous than any other type as a
means of transport, but because it is the most effective on
the road and the machine of choice for cycle enthusiasts.

Historically, cycling has been both a means of self-powered transport and a recreational activity. The urge to travel far and fast has driven the development of the road bike from its origins in the late 19th century and the early days of the safety bicycle as, first, racing cyclists and their hard-riding imitators and, later, progressive cycle tourists and club riders sought to extract even more performance from the limited means at their disposal.

The road bike, as distinct from the utility roadster, can be traced back to the introduction in the 1920s of an improved style of frame construction and of components in aluminium alloys, and in the 1930s of high-tensile steel frame tubing. But even before these dates, the resources of the cycle manufacturing industry were pushing the boundaries of cycle design in search of the perfect human-powered vehicle.

The result is the road bike in its many and varied guises. It is not an invention as such, but the culmination of any number of inventions or developments. Exotic early derailleur gear mechanisms and centre-pull brake calipers may be unlamented but undoubtedly played an important part in the ongoing development of the machine that today enjoys the appreciation its unique combination of qualities has long deserved.

Although any bicycle can be ridden on the road, the term 'road bike' is usually reserved for a type of machine that prioritises performance, if not outright speed, over mere utility. Therefore, it is unsurprising that road bikes are widely associated with cycle road racing and indeed it could be argued that the description 'road bike' is simply a convenient abbreviation for 'road-racing bike'. However, most bicycles styled and equipped along the lines of competition road bikes are used for fast leisure riding or for taking part in the currently booming cyclo-sportive scene. They often feature a more upright, relaxed riding position than would be adopted for serious competition.

Many questions are raised about the performance of the road bike. For example, does a road bike need multiple gears? Since a convincing argument can be made for using a fixed-wheel transmission on the grounds of economy or efficiency or even as an aid to training, then the answer has to be no. Another question might be whether the road bike should be 'stripped down for racing' or whether mudguards can be fitted. But in actuality, a racing bike with clip-on mudguards is no less of a road bike than one without.

Racing, touring and leisure cyclists appreciate the heightened performance of a bicycle set up to make the most of the human engine. In essence, the road bike is a fast- and easy-running machine with ergonomics suitable for a wide range of riding conditions. More specifically, it is a lightweight cycle equipped with dropped handlebars, narrow(ish) tyres and an efficient connection between feet and pedals. However it is defined, here's to the road bike; the finest machine on the road.

Anatomy of a Bike

Elegant and uncluttered, the bicycle exposes all but its innermost workings to the onlooker's admiring gaze and every component is designed and styled with this in mind. The result is invariably a visual delight that is only enhanced by an intimate knowledge of the machine and its constituent parts.

1. Saddle
2. Seat rails
3. Seatpost clamp
4. Brake cable
5. Top tube
6. Handlebars
7. Brake hoods
8. Levers
9. Adjusting barrel
10. Fork crown
11. Fork blade
12. Hub
13. Front dropout
14. Valve stem
15. Pedal
16. Crank arm
17. Down tube
18. Front derailleur
19. Crankset
20. Chainring
21. Seat post
22. Chain
23. Chainstay
24. Tyre
25. Rim
26. Wheel
27. Rear derailleur
28. Rear dropout
29. Spoke
30. Cassette
31. Seatstay
32. Brake pad
33. Brake caliper
34. Seatpost

1

Materials

The materials used to build the modern lightweight road bike are some of the finest available: from ultra-high modulus carbon-fibre to heat-treatable 6000-series aluminium alloys and 6Al-4V titanium alloy. Any suggestion that they have pushed an old favourite, steel, to the margins can be dismissed; the latest low-alloy steel tubes remain a convincing contender at any level of road cycling activity short of elite racing.

Materials: Overview

There are many materials in a lightweight road bike – the list includes rubbers, high-strength synthetic fibres, moulded hard plastics, elastic polymers, ethylene vinyl acetate (EVA) foam, Teflon and synthetic or natural leather – and it would be a major engineering challenge to build as effective a machine without them. The materials that interest the road cyclist the most, however, are those of which frames, forks and other substantial parts are made: carbon-fibre composites, steel, titanium and aluminium.

Carbon-fibre, steel, titanium and aluminium are all 'strong' materials, but strength is generally less of an issue than another material property, which is stiffness, or resistance to deflection. Measured by a figure known as Young's modulus, this stiffness varies with material; the higher the modulus, the stiffer the material and the less it will stretch under a given load.

Steel, which has a modulus three times greater than that of aluminium, may sound like the better material for a bike frame. In fact, as steel is three times denser than aluminium, the stiffness-to-weight ratio, or specific modulus, is almost exactly matched.

As aluminium is one third the weight of steel, three times the amount can be used in making a component of the same weight. The larger cross-sectional area gives it much greater bending stiffness and this geometric effect means that the same is true of tubes as of solid bars: the bending stiffness of a tube of a given wall thickness increases in proportion to the cube of its radius. A tube of heavy old steel must either have a very thin wall susceptible to buckling or a small diameter. Whereas an aluminium tube 1.5 times the diameter with twice the wall thickness will weigh about the same but be more than twice as stiff in bending and even more in torsion.

This comparative shortfall means that steel's much greater strength is of no benefit if maximising stiffness is the aim. The same is true of titanium but the area effect allows titanium, at just over half the weight and half the stiffness, to compete with steel on ride comfort. By playing around with a small increase in tube diameter and with wall thickness, a titanium tube can be made as stiff as steel but lighter, or less stiff and the same weight, as desired.

Steel-tube cycle frames stayed at the top of the performance tree for as long as they did because the technology needed when working with aluminium and titanium took a long time in development. As soon as they were outclassed, steel bike frames went almost immediately and have only recently regained some ground. Fans of the more traditional steel may take comfort from the thought that titanium, seen at one time as the ultimate material for lightweight cycles, has barely figured in professional bike racing while aluminium did not stay at the top for very long, quickly falling from favour in the face of something even better suited to lightweight cycle frame construction: carbon-fibre composite.

Carbon-fibre is the automatic choice for anyone wanting the lightest, stiffest bike material possible. The demand for components in carbon-fibre, easily the most desirable material in cycle construction, keeps design engineers busy.

Carbon-fibre

Carbon-fibre is the go-to material for high-end cycle construction; parts made in carbon-fibre are usually lighter and stiffer than anything else. To work to its best advantage, carbon-fibre design needs space to put the fibres where they can best resist the stresses of cycling. It is ideal for large, hollow structures such as aero wheel rims, frame spars and the front fork where its weight and stiffness advantage over metals can be used to create complex wall shapes otherwise impossible or possible only with a considerable weight penalty.

Steel

The oldest of the major structural materials used in the road bike's frame, steel is often lauded as somehow 'real', unlike lighter materials. It is worth consideration where saving every last gramme is not a major factor of choice. Steel is also used in many bike parts: hardened chromium steels are used for bearing balls and races and high-tensile stainless steel wire for spokes and control cable inner wire. Smaller rear derailleur sprockets rely on steel's hardness for their longevity; steel pedal axles outperform titanium on any cost basis and, while heavier, flex less.

Titanium

Tough, light, exceptionally strong for its weight, corrosion resistant and blessed with a subtle natural colouring that looks equally good brushed, polished or bead-blasted, titanium has all the attributes of the perfect frame-building material. It is, however, difficult to produce, hard to manipulate and tricky to machine without taking great care to avoid galling; it was also hard to join until tungsten inert gas (TIG) welding became widely used.

Aluminium

Given aluminium's low weight and the fact that its high specific strength can exceed that of some alloy steels, it is, perhaps, surprising that aluminium alloys failed to make a notable impact on road bike frame construction until the mid-1990s. Although their stay at the top of the sport was brief, aluminium frames remain popular at the lower-priced end of the road bike market thanks to their high performance-to-cost ratio.

Carbon-Fibre

Apparent from the 1960s, carbon-fibre's potential began to be realised in the 1980s by the French firm Technique du Verre Tissé (TVT) and early frames, comprising carbon-fibre tubes bonded into aluminium lugs, were raced at professional level by the Peugeot and La Vie Claire cycle teams.

Weight

Unidirectional fibre is increasingly used in preference to twill or weave to improve stiffness; instead of interweaving, the fibres of each unidirectional layer run straight and provide maximum resistance to tensile stress.

Most manufacturers use pre-preg sheets, in which the fibres are supplied impregnated with a thermo-setting resin. It is convenient but requires care when placing cut sections of sheet in the mould and can trap air within the composite matrix. TIME uses a technique known as Resin Transfer Molding (RTM), where 'dry' fibres, usually pre-woven as a tubular sock, are placed within male and female moulds as resin is injected under pressure, replacing the air around the fibres and filling any voids.

Using these and other, as yet undisclosed, manufacturing techniques, the leading manufacturers have succeeded in shaving the weight of a frame and fork to less than 1kg, although 1100g is a good ballpark figure.

Frame construction

The mid-1990s saw frame builders large and small test various ways to use carbon-fibre. Progress was rapid; Colnago's C40 frame, supplied originally with a steel fork and disguised to look like bonded aluminium, carried Swiss road racing cyclist Tony Rominger through the mountains to victory in the 1993 Vuelta a España and won five times over the cobbles of Paris-Roubaix, including the Italian racing team Mapei's famous '1-2-3' of 1996.

The C40's construction method comprised carbon-fibre tubes bonded into lugs of the same material, which were made in collaboration with Ferrari. Introduced by pioneer Craig Calfee, the method allows the building of a wide range of frame sizes without the need for numerous expensive monocoque moulds, relying on a series of smaller moulds for each of the lug 'suites' required to build a particular frame size. The lugged-and-bonded technique was also used by firms such as TIME Sport International, France, and is noted for producing light frames with a supple ride quality. An alternative, used by smaller frame builders such as Billato, Italy, joins tubes by means of carbon-fibre twill wrapped around the junctions and compacted using air pressure.

Monocoque, or single-piece, construction has proven less adaptable than the semi-monocoque technique. Instead of one large moulding, the frame is made in several smaller components bonded together. The finished frame is structurally similar to a true monocoque but dimensional accuracy is easier to control and the manufacturer can save on costs by using one section for more than one frame size.

▼ The lightest and stiffest material available for frame and fork construction, carbon-fibre is the first choice for competition cycles.

Steel

When it comes to the construction of bike frames, steel sets the standard for ride, handling and that intangible 'feel' that is impossible to measure but undoubtedly possible to discern. The feel of steel derives from the invention of tube butting by Alfred Reynolds in 1897.

Durability

Provided rust is not allowed to get a grip, a steel frame is durable. Small dents and surface imperfections, which would render a lightweight aluminium frame suspect, rarely have a detrimental effect. Then there is the ease of manufacture and repair: steel tubes can be brazed, welded and bonded. Bespoke frame building is possible and small details such as the filing of a rear dropout or the delicate tapering of a hand finished lug offer an appeal unavailable with other materials.

The latest stainless steel cast lugs and fork crowns will take a mirror polish, as will high strength stainless steel tubesets from Columbus and Reynolds. The results far outshine the bulked-up, bulbous, bare spars of a carbon-fibre Pro Tour team bike or the matted sheen of brushed titanium and prove that, while steel may be old-school, it is not old hat.

Frame construction

Butting adds extra strength to the frame tubes where it is required; the walls of a butted tube are thicker at the ends, where the bending stresses during riding are greatest and where the tubes are heated during the building process, than in the middle (see p. 36). This saves weight in comparison to a frame built with non-butted 'plain gauge' tubes and makes for a more resilient tube, since it can deflect more while offering the same overall strength.

Lightweight steel frame tubes improved steadily with the development of improved low-alloy steels by firms such as Accles and Pollock, and Reynolds. By the mid-1920s, frames built using Reynolds high-manganese tubes and joined using improved brazing and silver brazing techniques offered near modern standards of weight, resilience and ride comfort. Newer materials are still judged by reference to the supposed qualities of a fine steel frame – although the weight difference between a carbon-fibre and a steel fork is so great that there needs to be a compelling reason to choose the latter on a new machine.

The latest top-end steel tubesets such as Columbus Spirit or Reynolds 953 build into a very light frame; close to 1.5kg (3.3 lbs) is possible. Even a second-tier tubeset can be built into a lightweight frame that will perform close to the level of a competent carbon-fibre or titanium offering.

Steel is springy in a way that compares favourably with both titanium and carbon-fibre. A well designed and built steel frame has a supple ride quality. The same is true of a steel fork; the inherent flex in a delicately raked blade takes out road vibration that gets past the front tyre, unmatched by all but the most high-tech of carbon-fibre forks.

▼ A highly polished finish gives frames built using the latest stainless steel tubesets an unmatched visual appeal.

Titanium

The first titanium road bike frame, weighing about 1.25kg (2.8lbs), was displayed by Phillips at the 1956 Cycle Show. Road cyclists then had to wait until 1972 to see a production titanium frame by Speedwell Gear Case Co., Birmingham; an example was ridden by Spanish cyclist Luis Ocaña in the 1973 Tour de France.

Frame construction

The Speedwell titanium frame was quickly followed by versions from German bike manufacturer Flema and the fabled Teledyne Titan from the US. The Teledyne frame was carefully designed to combat titanium's known deficiency when compared to steel and it featured slightly oversized tubes to add stiffness. Its titanium fork and slender rear stays ensured that the Teledyne provided a 'comfortable' ride, but it suffered from random breakages just as the US bike boom of the day came to an end.

Regarded as soft, expensive and fragile, titanium bikes faded from the public imagination until the mid-1980s when the metal's reputation was rescued by US firms Merlin Metalworks and Litespeed. The first to manufacture road bike frames using butted titanium tubes, Merlin also built the first using the important 3Al–2.5V titanium alloy, which forms the bulk of production today.

Raced by American road cyclist Greg LeMond and his Z Team in the 1991 Tour de France, the Merlin Extra Light realised the material's potential. By this time Litespeed had built enough of a reputation for titanium fabrication and welding that Italian frame building maestro Irio Tommasini sent a craftsman to the factory to find out how it was done.

Titanium's glory years followed as teams such as the French GAN rode titanium road and time trial bikes on the European professional race scene, and titanium gurus such as Scot Nicol of the US Ibis created an aura of exclusivity around high cost frames. The peak hit in 1998, when Swiss cyclist Alex Zuelle raced a Litespeed Vortex in the Tour de France and US contender Lance Armstrong rode the same firm's Blade in that year's world time trial championship.

Pricing

Within a few years, titanium stopped being the pro racer's choice on performance grounds and prices slumped as low cost frames from Eastern Europe and China arrived. Its special qualities remain, however, and a number of smaller companies have steadily rebuilt its reputation.

The high cost of titanium until the end of the 1990s ensured that titanium frames remained for the well-heeled while the aura of the US brands deterred small scale producers from entering the market. With the drop in the cost of raw materials and rising demand, firms such as Enigma, UK, and Van Nicholas, Netherlands, have since broadened titanium's appeal by building anything from touring bikes to full-on racing machines. Enigma's entry into bespoke manufacture has put the titanium frame buyer in the same position as one looking at steel; able to specify the small details that make a road bike more than simply a fine high performance machine.

▼ Durable, comfortable and attractive, titanium is no longer the exotic material of the 1990s and appeals to tourists and sporting riders alike.

Aluminium

The usefulness of aluminium was revealed during the earliest days of safety bicycle construction: a cast aluminium frame and other parts were made in France in the 1890s. One third the density of steel and easy to cast, forge, machine and extrude, aluminium's suitability was obvious but was matched by the difficulty of making and joining reliable parts.

Frame construction

Aluminium's use in lightweight touring cycles took off in earnest in the 1930s as progressive builders in France and elsewhere increasingly used it to make frames and smaller parts such as wheel hubs and rims and brake calipers. At the time, aluminium or 'light' alloy was hard to join by any but mechanical means and methods employed to join frame tubes included crimping them around or threading them into lugs and even pinning. Gas welding was possible but required great skill, dissuading all but the most enterprising of frame builders from using aluminium at a time when great strides were being made with steel frames.

By the 1970s, two aluminium race bike framesets worthy of note were available: both the ALAN and Vitus 979 Duralinox designs used thick-walled aluminium tubes of standard external diameter screwed and bonded to hefty cast alloy lugs. Those of the ALAN frame, which enjoyed cyclo-cross success, were on the outside while those of the Vitus, raced with great distinction by Irish cyclist Sean Kelly, fitted the inside of the tubes. Their weight was comparable to that of a steel frameset, the ride stiff and longevity debatable.

Revered as the 'Sorcerer' by French enthusiasts, André Sablière began building gas-welded Zicral and 5000-series aluminium frames of stunning beauty in the early 1970s. At much the same time in the US, builders such as Gary Klein began TIG-welding oversized heat-treated 6000-series aluminium tubes to build frames notably stiffer, if no lighter than, contemporary steel designs and proved that aluminium, correctly handled, could outperform steel on stiffness while offering acceptable durability.

Stiffness

It was only a matter of time before aluminium replaced steel for competition. Sadly, within two years of German cyclist Jan Ullrich's 1997 Tour de France win on a Pinarello Paris, aluminium was superseded by carbon-fibre. No longer at the cutting edge of frame technology, aluminium is widely perceived to build into a stiff and uncomfortable frame that lacks sophistication. Unfortunately, overall 'stiffness' is one of the inherent characteristics of its resistance to fatigue. Since aluminium alloys have a finite fatigue life, limiting flex is the easiest way to ensure the frame's durability.

Aluminium road bikes make up a large proportion of the total number of bikes sold because they provide value for money; a good aluminium frame may not ride as sweetly as titanium, but it will be competitive on weight and less expensive. Steel frames offer a different experience and, in the case of low-cost steel frames, a markedly inferior one. Aluminium road bikes are the affordable face of performance cycling; long may they remain so.

▼ Aluminium's days at the summit of cycle sport are in the past but its combination of light weight and low cost ensures it remains a popular choice with road cyclists.

2

Frameset

A frameset is the foundation on which the rest of the cycle is built. It is made up of the frame and its fork, and informs every aspect of performance from handling to power transfer. The standard diamond bicycle frame design is a masterful and simple piece of engineering that has stood the test of time, its shape dictated by the twin constraints of structural integrity and the regulations governing cycle racing.

Frameset Evolution

The conventional, classic road bike's diamond frame design is elegant and simple, and is a good example of careful compromise in the search for structural efficiency. The diamond shape is used almost universally because it works: it is effectively composed of two triangles (the stiffest shape for a tubular structure) laid side-on. It isn't perfect, but with the application of composite materials and computer-aided structural analysis to its layout it comes very close.

Early form

The front-wheel-driven bicycle had a single-spar connection between steering head and rear wheel fork. This made sense as there was no need to support the pedal axle bearings separately from the wheel. With one or two unsuccessful exceptions, the earliest safety bicycles took a broadly similar path in connecting the two wheels by means of a steerable front fork and single spar leading to a rigid rear fork. The problem of locating the seat and pedal axle was addressed by placing the two at opposite ends of a single tubular spar that crossed the main backbone just ahead of the rear wheel fork.

▼ The triangulation of the diamond frame confers exceptional strength and stiffness; in comparison, the cross frame concentrates stresses at the junction of a series of struts, requiring extra material to provide the required strength.

Cross frame

The cross-frame layout typified by the Rudge Bicyclette of 1888 could be described as structurally poor. Beyond that, it offered little resistance to vertical distortion due to the limited strength of the tubes at the crossing point. Meanwhile, the highly loaded bottom bracket housing for the crank axle enjoyed little support and was free to deflect in any direction, but downwards, under pedalling loads. The frame's resistance to breakage derived almost entirely from the thickness of its tube walls, especially in the area of the main cross junction. The thick walls needed to provide adequate strength also added to any cross-frame weight that could be ill afforded.

There was a way in which the layout made sense, not merely in terms of simplicity but structurally. It was almost invariably braced against distortion by a thin tension rod slung between the bottom bracket and the steering head. On the poor road surfaces of the day, this afforded the frame a degree of suspension and enough vertical flex to absorb some of the vibration that made its way past the solid rubber examples that preceded the application of pneumatic tyres.

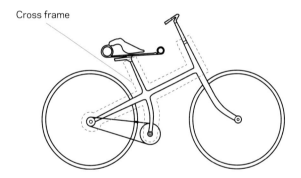

Diamond frame

Cross frame

THE WHIPPET

The 'Whippet' design by UK cycle engineers Lindley and Biggs employed springs placed above and below the backbone to control its movement relative to the seat tube, which was separate from the backbone but connected by stays to the bottom bracket and rear wheel hub. The seat tube was attached to the bottom bracket and to a spar locating the handlebar, which turned the front wheel through a scissors shackle. The layout of this ingenious machine ensured that the wheels could move independently of the seat, bottom bracket and handlebars, which were kept fixed in relation to each other.

The limited torsional rigidity of the cross frame was of little consequence given the relatively slow progress that could be achieved on one of these machines. Their appeal was to the safety minded bicyclist of the day; with solid-tyred wheels of smaller diameter than the driving wheel of an ordinary 'penny-farthing' bicycle, with the exception of the 'Whippet' and similar spring-framed cycles, they were slower and less comfortable.

Diamond frame

With the successful introduction of the pneumatic tyre (see p. 63), the ordinary bicycle – such as the high-wheeler or 'penny-farthing' bicycle – was doomed. No longer did the small wheels of the safety bicycle hinder its progress or create uncomfortable vibration on rough roads. The pneumatic tyre was tried on the ordinary but, tellingly, any advantage it conferred was minimal and probably outweighed by the problem of the puncture. Tellingly, too, the rapid uptake of the pneumatic tyre coincided almost exactly with the demise of the cross frame; with air cushioning available to absorb vibration, the vertical stiffness of the diamond frame was of no consequence while its structural soundness allowed engineers to whittle away at excess material.

Introduced in 1890, the Humber safety featured true diamond construction as well as recognisably modern features such as ball-element steering bearings, similar size wheels and adjustable seat height. Its superiority in terms of strength, stiffness and weight over the competition, which included both cross-frame and non-diamond designs, was such that the layout was, within five years, the industry standard.

While the diamond frame appears to be made of two conjoined triangles, the front 'triangle' is an irregular quadrilateral or trapezoid with, usually, a very short tube at the steering head. Depending on the length of the head tube, the front triangle is able to deflect under vertical load in a way that it would not if a perfect triangle. The resulting increase in vertical flexibility is highly desirable as can be seen from the many efforts made by cycle manufacturers to engineer additional vertical flex, or 'compliance', into the road bike frame.

▲ The designers of early cross frames showed great ingenuity in trying to strengthen their designs.

Despite its dominance, the diamond frame was not left unchallenged in the years after its emergence. Surely the most singular and easily the most effective of the alternatives was patented by Mikael Pedersen, a Danish engineer living in Dursley, Gloucestershire, in 1893. Seeking to improve on the comfort of the regular leather bicycle saddle, Pedersen invented a hammock saddle constructed of cord netting and then designed a frame and fork to accommodate it. His frame was entirely triangulated, leaving the paired small-diameter tubes subjected to either tension or

ROVER SAFETY BIKE

Preceding the explosion in the popularity of the cross frame at the end of the 1880s, James Starley's Rover safety bicycle of 1885 was based on a frame that came close to the diamond layout thanks to the provision of seat and chainstays along with top and down tubes. Its lozenge or open-diamond shape lacked only a seat tube, perhaps to save weight. The addition of a triangulating seat tube to the lozenge made it stiffer and stronger, especially in the vertical plane. This, in turn, allowed tubes and the lugs that joined them to be made with thinner, lighter walls.

compression loads only, and was exceptionally light for the time. Its complexity and consequent cost told against it, however, as did its poor lateral rigidity.

Although other frame types appeared over the following decades, none seriously challenged the standard diamond layout for use in lightweight road bikes until the end of the 20th century. Even then, the successful challenger (once composite beam frames had been banned from competition) was a variation on the theme rather than something substantially different. Drawing on mountain bike practice and benefiting from the growing availability of extra-long seat posts, a number of cycle designers began to tweak the shape of the diamond, shortening the seat tube and altering the angle of the now-sloping top tube and seatstays to suit. Trumpeted by the Taiwanese firm Giant, the world's largest cycle manufacturer, as a way to reduce the number of stock frame sizes required to fit the various-sized members of the cycling population, the 'compact' frame has, in some market sectors, almost entirely displaced the conventional horizontal top tube diamond frame. Ignoring any claims for sizing convenience, the compact layout does offer some advantages: the top tube is shorter for a given frame size, saving weight and adding torsional stiffness, the main 'triangle' becomes a flatter irregular quadrilateral, making it easier to deflect vertically, and the seat post is longer and more flexible.

Whether built with a horizontal or sloping top tube, the diamond frame offers the best combination of vertical, torsional and lateral strength and stiffness, weight, component location and ease of manufacture of any of the possible layouts. And, somehow, it looks right. It will be with us for a long time.

▼ 'Compact' frame geometry is typified by a sloping top tube and extended seat post and has been almost universally adopted for road bikes.

Frameset: Tubes

A diamond bicycle frame is essentially a simple assembly. It is composed, at its most basic, of eight tubes, a bottom bracket shell and dropouts – or 'ends' – for the rear wheel. However, it is an elegant structure that cleverly reconciles the demands imposed on it in ways that can be affected by parameters such as the joining of the tubes, the material the tubes are made of and the purpose of the completed bicycle.

1. Seatstays
2. Seat tube
3. Top tube
4. Head tube
5. Down tube
6. Bottom bracket
7. Chainstays
8. Dropouts

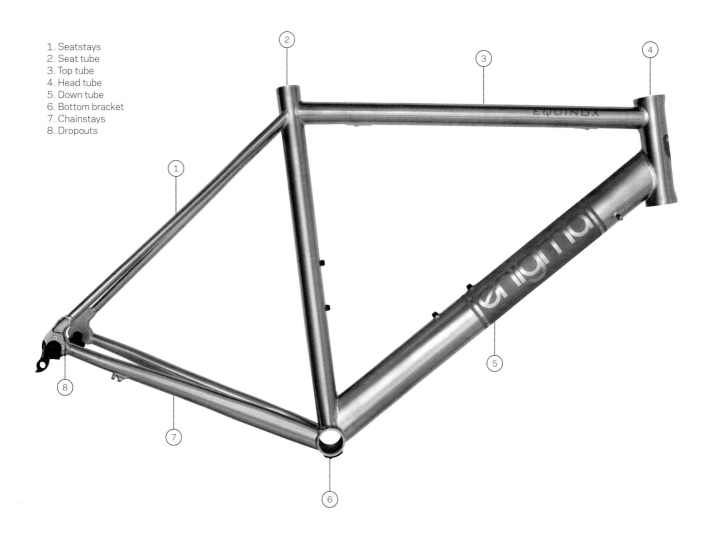

Head tube

At the front of the frame sits the head tube. Although it has a fairly easy life – being short, stout and subject to little by way of bending stresses – its design specifics have a big effect on the way the bike works. Its prominent location also makes the head tube the perfect location for a maker's badge or logo.

The head tube's most demanding task is that of locating the lower of the two steering, or head, bearings, which transfers the major part of the loads generated by the front fork to the frame. Irrespective of the type of head bearing (see pp. 46–47) it takes, the head tube is traditionally of constant diameter inside and out along its length, and the internal ends of the tube must be reamed before the top and bottom headset cups can be pressed in place.

Tube length

While many cyclists favour the visible presence of the external headset bearing, others find pleasing the sleek appearance made possible by the integrated headset, which situates the upper and lower bearings in recesses cut directly into the head tube. In this case, the head tube will be longer – by the depth of the headset – than one that takes an external headset.

It is vital, when considering head tube length as an aspect of frame sizing, to confirm the type of head bearing used in the frame. On a cycle with threadless head bearings, head tube length determines minimum handlebar height. A head tube that is long in relation to the top tube will put the handlebars at a height that suits the more relaxed road rider and is a reliable signifier of a bike intended for sportive or endurance riding.

In search of maximum front-end stiffness, the most aggressive current competition road frames use a super, oversized lower head bearing designed to fit a tapered steerer tube with 38.1mm (1.5in) outer diameter (OD) at the fork crown. The head tube must be shaped accordingly and be wider at the bottom, giving the cycle a sturdy air that may or may not appeal to the onlooker.

TUBE RESISTANCE

For a given mass of material, a round-section tube is the shape best at resisting bending and twisting loads applied from a range of directions. The thinner the tube walls, the stiffer and, up to a point, stronger it will be. A tube with very thin walls will crumple when overloaded in compression. This practical limit to tube wall thickness also restricts the tube diameter that can be reached within a given weight limit.

Aerodynamics

Sitting at the front of the cycle, the head tube travels through undisturbed air, making it a prime candidate for profiling to improve aerodynamics. Experiments in this field go back as far as 1979, when French manufacturer Gitane built a cycle with a teardrop-shaped head tube for cyclist Bernard Hinault. The five-time Tour de France winner rode the bike to victory in that year's Grand Prix des Nations time trial and later rode it in time trials during the Tour itself. The classic teardrop head tube profile, which has appeared on many machines since, is now being replaced by a truncated airfoil shape such as the Kamm Virtual Foil (KVF) of US manufacturer Trek's Madone KVF model (see p. 39) in order to comply with regulations governing competition cycles.

▼ The head tube is the traditional site for a maker's badge. It may bulge outwards to provide the space for integrated head bearings.

Top tube

Connecting the top of the head tube and the top of the seat tube, the top tube usually houses the cable for the rear brake.

Rear brake cable

Engineering, as much as design considerations, tends to dictate the way the cable is routed. Back when it was considered unwise to heat lightweight steel tubes unless necessary, the cable's uninterrupted outer casing would be attached to the top tube using chromed steel clips. As it became accepted practice to silver-braze small parts to low-alloy steel tubes, the outer casing was usually passed through brazed-on guides on the top of the tube. Nowadays, the outer casing is broken by stops brazed to the tube, giving a firmer braking action by replacing slightly compressible casing with less compressible frame tube.

Hiding the cable inside the frame is an attractive design feature, but requires two openings to be made in the tube, either adding weight, if reinforced, or creating a weak point. The ease with which openings for an internally routed cable can be safely made without adding weight to a carbon-fibre frame has given designers a free hand with hiding cables inside its tubes.

Tube width

In structural terms the top tube does less work than the down tube and is slightly smaller in diameter. Nevertheless, it makes an important contribution to the frame's torsional stiffness and therefore affects handling. This has led to a vogue in carbon-fibre and aluminium frame design for ever wider and stiffer top tubes as frame designers aim to retain stiffness while saving weight. Excessive top tube width is a potential problem for the many cyclists who naturally pedal with their knees close to the tube.

FRAME GEOMETRY

A frame's geometry describes the various angles and dimensions that determine its size and ride quality. The two important angles are those of the head and seat tubes; for a mid-size road frame, angles of around 73° are usual for both.

Bottom bracket height determines how far the rider's centre of gravity sits above the ground and how much pedal clearance is available when cornering. Frame size was traditionally decided by the length of the seat tube but current practice is to go by a combination of top tube length and head tube height to find the best fit.

Wheelbase is the distance between tyre contact points with the ground and is affected by parameters including chainstay and top tube lengths, frame angles and fork rake. In general, a shorter wheelbase makes for a lighter, stiffer bike with more responsive handling; a longer wheelbase confers greater stability and ride comfort.

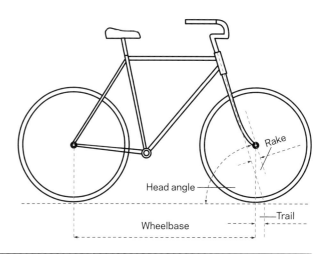

Down tube

Connecting the head tube and bottom bracket shell, the down tube has to contend with forces generated by pedalling, braking, steering and cornering and takes up much of a frame designer's attention. It is traditionally fatter by one eighth of an inch than the top tube but can be made much more substantial in pursuit of improved performance – and a larger billboard for the company name.

Tube width

Perhaps the first manufacturer to grasp the structural importance of the down tube was Cannondale. In the 1990s, the Bedford, Connecticut, firm came up with the idea of the Power Pyramid, which was first realised on the 2.8 road frame in the form of a conical down tube that increased in diameter as it approached the bottom bracket shell. The smaller-diameter head tube end had thicker tube walls for strength at this highly stressed junction.

Since then, many forms and profiles have been applied to the down tube, some of them seemingly chosen more for their impressive appearance than any tangible performance advantage. The development of the hydro-forming process for shaping aluminium tubes has also allowed designers to create forms previously only feasible if moulded in carbon-fibre and the down tube is the perfect canvas for their art.

Cable stoppage

Bosses for gear cable stops are usually situated on the forward sides or undersides of the tube and, increasingly, house a threaded adjuster screw. Handbuilt steel frames may employ a pair of square-sided braze-on pieces originally designed to work with down-tube-mounted derailleur shift levers. They also accept small aluminium or plastic bosses complete with adjuster screws that work with handlebar-mounted shift levers.

▼ Threaded adjusters situated on the down tube allow derailleur gear indexing adjustment 'on the fly'.

Seat tube

Like the down tube, the seat tube is often used as the location for braze-on bottle cage bosses. It also locates the front derailleur mechanism fitted using either a braze-on slotted bracket fixed permanently to the tube, or a band that clamps to the tube. The band can only be used on a round tube of constant diameter so the bracket – which must be accurately positioned – is the mount of choice on many carbon-fibre and aluminium frames with curvaceous seat tubes. On these, it is usually riveted in place, although some high-end carbon-fibre frames now save weight with a carbon-fibre bracket bonded in position.

Frame flex

The seat tube completes the structure of the diamond frame and, at its lower end, supports the bottom bracket shell against flex. A variety of means have been tried to increase its effectiveness: the Italian firm Bianchi tried injecting 'structural' foam to the base of the seat tube of its late-1990s Mega Pro XL aluminium race bike to combat flex-induced fatigue. Cannondale's Power Pyramid label now applies to the seat tube of the 2014 Synapse Carbon Hi-MOD. The tube splits in two above the bracket shell, splaying out to meet the sides and support the shell without adding weight.

► Cinelli's classic Supercorsa frame has a 'fastback' seatstay arrangement with the clamp bolt passing through the seatstays below an inlaid pearl logo.

BUTTING

Butted tubes have walls that are thicker at the ends, where extra strength is needed and where the tubes are heated during the building process. This not only saves weight in comparison to a frame built with non-butted 'plain-gauge' tubes but makes for a more resilient, 'livelier' frame since the stresses in the tube are better distributed along its length.

A tube may be single-butted, meaning it has thicker walls at only one end, or double-butted. The seat tube is usually butted at the heavily stressed bottom bracket end but not at the top, where loads are lighter and the seat lug or cluster provides support.

Steel cycle tubes are internally butted using a process that involves drawing the tube through a die of exact dimensions. It has a shaped mandrel inside that is extracted by twisting the tube between rollers to compress it lengthways, widening it enough to pop the mandrel out.

Due to the metal's toughness, external butting is widely used for titanium cycle frame tubes. The tube is usually placed over a press-fitted mandrel and the outside either machined on a CNC lathe or ground to leave the tube's ends with thicker walls than its middle.

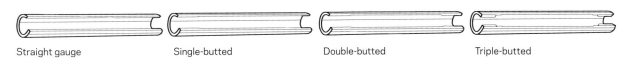

| Straight gauge | Single-butted | Double-butted | Triple-butted |

Seat tube angle

Placing the seat some way behind the bottom bracket axle, the seat tube angle varies according to frame size and, in a handbuilt frame, the personal requirements of the customer. Current road bike practice usually sets it at between 72° and 74°. The almost universal road bike practice is to make the centre line of the tube intersect with the bottom bracket axle so that the seat angle remains constant as the seat height is changed.

Most road bikes employ a seat tube cut off at the top of or immediately above the seat lug or cluster and use a seat post that slides inside to allow seat height and alignment to be adjusted. The post should be a snug enough fit to stay in place without being held by hand and is usually secured in place by a bolt that pulls the tube tightly around the post. The bolt may act directly on 'ears' brazed to the tube or incorporated within the seat lug or it may work through a separate band placed over the exposed end of the tube.

Weight can be saved by extending the seat tube beyond the seat cluster as a mast, dispensing with the seat post and opting for a seat clamp that fits directly over the mast. This layout creates problems with seat height adjustment and applies substantial stress to the base of the mast; better is the system adopted by Trek, which extends the seat tube as a short stub above the cluster over which a moveable cap slides.

Dropouts

Behind the seat tube lies the rear triangle, which is, in fact, composed of two triangles, one either side of the rear wheel. Each is, in turn, made up of a seat and a chainstay with a rear dropout, or 'end' at the apex. Invented by French racer and engineer Eugène Christophe, the dropout is so called because, unlike a rear-opening 'track end' as used in a track racing bike and some fixed-wheel or single-speed machines, it allows the rear wheel axle to move forward before dropping out of the frame. Christophe realised that this would make wheel removal quicker and easier by obviating the need to unship the drive chain from the rear wheel sprocket beforehand.

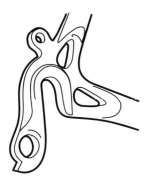

▲ Vertical dropout

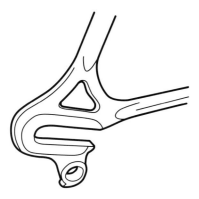

▲ Long dropout
▶

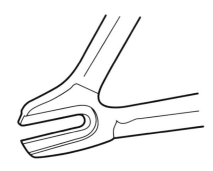

▲ Track end

Form and function

The slot of a track end is parallel to the ground to preserve bottom bracket height as the rear wheel is moved to adjust chain slack. A long slot allowing plenty of rear wheel adjustment was a feature of road bike dropouts until the 1980s, when frame builders began to adopt the vertical dropout. As its name implies, this design allows the wheel to drop straight down to exit the frame. It greatly speeds wheel installation and makes for a stiffer rear end but, as no fore-and-aft wheel adjustment is possible, requires more accuracy in building to ensure the wheel sits centrally between the stays. It also requires a derailleur or other chain tensioning mechanism to take up slack and is, therefore, unsuitable for use with a fixed-wheel or single-speed transmission (see pp. 122–123).

Material

Road bike dropout design has progressed over several decades in tandem with material usage to the point where top-flight carbon-fibre frames use moulded carbon-fibre dropouts weighing perhaps 35g (1.2oz) each. A replaceable derailleur gear hanger is commonplace although some argue that, being weaker, such a feature is more likely to bend and need replacement than a solid hanger.

Steel dropouts are usually forged to shape while titanium examples are mostly laser-cut or CNC-machined to shape. Aluminium dropouts can be made in several ways including cutting from sheet metal and cold-forging and, because the metal is so light, can be made with a thick cross-section for added rigidity and to provide extra surface area for bonding or welding.

Seatstays and chainstays

The layout of the rear triangle, which approximates to a very slender tetrahedron, is so effective a structure that the stays need only be of slender cross-section. The seatstays, which need only resist the small bending loads generated by using the rear brake and the compression stresses from the weight of the rider, can be very delicate indeed.

The bridge between the seatstays is used to hold the rear brake. However, the latest Trek Madone KVF omits the bridge and puts the brake under the chainstays in search of lower aerodynamic drag. The chainstays must provide a connection between the bottom bracket shell and rear wheel stiff enough to resist the massive forces imposed by pedalling and are invariably much more substantial. Early versions of Cervélo's R3 road bike had chainstays so stiff that they theoretically rendered the frame's seatstays redundant.

Steel stays

Steel chainstays are usually stiff enough for the task. They are made in a variety of shapes of varying visual appeal, which is surely the best basis on which to make a selection.

Carbon-fibre stays

Much work has gone into shaping the chainstays of carbon-fibre frames in pursuit of the best balance of weight and stiffness and the current trend is to wrap the stays as closely around the tyre as possible while extending the bottom bracket shell rearwards to create a massively stiff box structure.

Titanium stays

Titanium frames may suffer from chainstay flex. The space available for the stays is limited by the width of the bottom bracket shell and, on the right-hand side, the proximity of the chainrings. The metal is tough and difficult to bend or manipulate into a shape that best utilises the space. Furthermore, since titanium is little over half as stiff as steel, a titanium stay needs walls twice as thick if it is to match a steel stay of the same shape. The answer is to use a heavy-gauge stay, but the right-hand chainstay remains titanium's Achilles heel.

Seatstay

Chainstay

▶ Trek's KVF Madone does not need a seatstay bridge as the rear brake sits under the chainstays.

JOINING

Carbon-fibre frame sections are joined by bonding, usually using strong two-part epoxy adhesives that offer excellent adhesion and durability. Low-alloy steel, stainless steel, titanium and aluminium can also be joined by bonding, which therefore allows carbon-fibre and metal parts to be joined together. Early carbon-fibre frames made by pioneering manufacturers such as TVT of France used carbon-fibre tubes bonded into aluminium lugs and the technique is still used when it is desired to employ, for example, carbon-fibre seatstays in a titanium frame.

Ideal for precision work, the Tungsten Inert Gas (TIG) welding process is the preferred means of welding metal cycle frame tubes and is used for steel, titanium and aluminium. An inert gas, usually argon, shields the weld pool from contamination by oxygen while the welding arc is struck between the work and a non-consumable tungsten electrode, melting the edges of the work pieces to create a weld pool. Filler rod of the same metal is added to the pool if needed; a titanium rod is required when welding titanium, an aluminium rod when welding aluminium and so on.

▼ TIG-welded ▼ Lugged joint ▼ Lugless joint

Bottom bracket

At the heart of the frame lies the bottom bracket shell. As incorporated in a state-of-the-art carbon-fibre frame it may simply refer to the general intersection of the down and seat tubes and chainstays around a point centred on the bottom bracket axle.

Shell form and function

A steel shell may have sockets into which fit the ends of the tubes and stays prior to brazing or a plain exterior if the joins are to be welded or fillet-brazed. Aluminium and titanium shells have a plain exterior suitable for welding to the various frame tubes.

The standard British-threaded road bike bottom bracket shell is 68mm wide and houses bearing cups with a 1.37 x 24 teeth per inch (tpi) thread. The right-hand cup has a left-hand thread to prevent it loosening as a result of annular precession, which makes the cup try to turn in the opposite direction to the rotation of the axle. The other common bottom bracket format is Italian; the shell is 70mm wide, has 36 x 24 tpi threads and uses a right-hand thread on both sides. The right-hand cup must be tightened with great force if it is not to come loose.

The shell diameter limits the size of bearing and therefore axle that can be fitted inside and several bottom bracket standards of recent invention aim to get around this. Cannondale's BB30 shell (see p. 102), for example, has an Internal Diameter (ID) of 41.96mm and accepts press-fitted 42mm OD 6806 format cartridge bearings, which permit the use of a beefy 30mm-diameter axle. Open to any manufacturer to use, the BB30 standard and its pressfit BB30 cousin have been widely adopted for use in carbon-fibre and aluminium frames. The weight of the large-diameter shell tells against its use in steel or titanium frames, however.

Sleeve

Manufacturers of carbon-fibre frames have tried many ways to solve the problem of locating the bottom bracket bearings. The most popular is to bond in place a metal – usually aluminium – sleeve threaded to accept the bearing cups. Another, used for BB30, Trek's BB90 and some other formats, is to form the shell with net-moulded carbon-fibre sockets that accept annular bearings pressed directly in place.

Derailleur cables are usually routed under the shell through low friction plastic guide channels. The vulnerable wiring for electronic shifters is, instead, routed through the inside of the frame and shell. Many road bike frames are now made in mechanical and electronic shifting-specific versions, avoiding the need to design a cable route that works well for both types of shift.

▼ Trek's proprietary BB90 bottom bracket design places the axle bearings in a massive box structure to maximise system rigidity.

Front Fork

Responsible for holding the front wheel, resisting the braking forces it generates, transmitting steering input and feedback and supporting a large part of the weight of bike and rider, the road bike's front fork has a lot of work to do. In fact, a well-designed fork does more, absorbing road shock and influencing favourably the way the bike handles and steers.

Construction materials

Steel, the preferred material for fork construction for most of cycling's history, has only recently been supplanted by carbon-fibre, which is now used for the majority of forks fitted to lightweight road bikes. Strong and stiff but 'springy', steel works well within the limited space of a standard inch-and-a-quarter head tube. Attempts to build titanium forks to fit standard road frames foundered on the issue of titanium's flexibility, since a titanium fork had to be either less rigid or heavier than steel.

Despite weighing much the same as a high-quality steel fork, all-aluminium forks made by ALAN and Vitus enjoyed some success for a brief period during the 1980s and early 1990s before disappearing as improvements in manufacturing technology made carbon-fibre forks lighter and more robust.

Forks with carbon-fibre blades and aluminium steerer tubes are now fitted to the majority of lightweight road bikes. While lighter than a competition steel fork, they are heavy compared to the best all-carbon designs, which can weigh as little as 320g.

Form and function

Whatever the material from which it is made, the road bike fork's overall layout is simplicity itself and was arrived at over 130 years ago. A steerer tube, or steerer, and two fork blades, each with an 'end' for the front wheel spindle, meet at a substantial crown. At the interface of the crown and steerer is a precision-cut or moulded seat for the head bearing's crown race.

The blades are cantilevered from the crown, which must be robust to counter the massive bending forces applied to it. The blades themselves are usually given a gentle taper so that they are broadest and stiffest at the crown end and are able to flex evenly along their length. Parallel-sided fork blades tend to transmit much more road shock to the highly loaded fork crown.

Fork rake may not be immediately obvious as many fork blades are straight and exit the crown at an angle to the steerer tube. Abandoned in the early years of safety bicycle development, straight blades were reintroduced in the Precisa fork by fabled Italian cycle manufacturer Ernesto Colnago, who claimed that they enhanced the fork's stiffness and therefore precision in sprints.

A straight fork blade takes a shorter path between wheel spindle and crown than does a curved one and is therefore both lighter and stiffer for a given blade cross-section and taper. Blades curved in the traditional manner to create fork rake flex more readily over road bumps, improve ride comfort, reduce loads applied to the crown and give the lower head bearing an easier life. Many cyclists consider them more visually appealing.

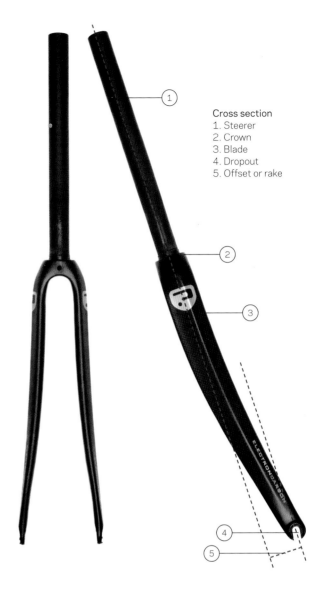

Cross section
1. Steerer
2. Crown
3. Blade
4. Dropout
5. Offset or rake

SAFETY TABS

Slots in the fork ends allow the wheel spindle to drop straight out when the wheel retention mechanism is loosened, unless 'safety' tabs are fitted. These small projections prevent the quick-release skewer nut and head from passing when the lever is flipped open; the nut must be unscrewed by several turns before the wheel will drop from the fork.

This feature, introduced to protect manufacturers from liability claims made by cyclists unable to use a quick-release lever correctly, hinders wheel removal unnecessarily as the quick-release concept has provided a reliable and secure means of wheel retention since its introduction by Tullio Campagnolo in 1930. The tabs also require the user to readjust the nut every time the wheel is installed, thus adding to the complexity of the task facing the inexperienced user.

Steerer tubes

The adoption of the oversized 1⅛in (28.6mm) steerer tube and headset format played its part in improving carbon-fibre fork performance. A 1⅛in steerer tube is over 40% stiffer than standard; even this is not enough for some manufacturers and the trend is towards steerer tubes that are fatter still at the crown but with a taper towards the top. Giant's OverDrive 2 system, for example, comprises a tapered steerer tube 1½in in diameter at the fork crown and tapering to 1¼in at the top end. The super-oversized steerer increases torsional rigidity by a claimed 30% without weight penalty but requires a handlebar stem with 1¼in clamp internal diameter.

Suitable for use with a standard 1⅛in stem's steerer clamp, Trek's E2 steerer tapers from 1⅛in in diameter at the fork crown. It also has another interesting feature; the steerer tube is ovalised with the longer axis aligned across the frame. This makes the steerer tube stiffer laterally and more flexible in the fore-and-aft plane, helping to absorb road shock without compromising on steering precision.

The almost universal move to the 1⅛in headset standard represents something of a quandary for the potential handbuilt steel frame buyer, since the massive increase in stiffness it conveys is of little consequence. A 1in steel steerer tube works perfectly well. However, it may be better, if ordering a new steel frameset, to opt for the larger format as it is easier to find threadless headsets and handlebar stems to suit.

Lightweight forks

Lightweight steel forks may not boast such refinement but they exhibit clever design. Conventional blades, for example, are shaped to give the frame builder the means to fine-tune their resilience. The taper extends for perhaps three quarters of the total blade length; beyond that the upper section of the blade is parallel-sided. The blade as supplied is, at 390mm, longer than needed for a road fork; before the blades are brazed to the crown, the excess is removed as required by the builder. If removed from the tapered end, this will leave the straight section longer, the more flexible tapered section shorter and the blade as a whole stiffer than would be the case if the excess was removed from the other end. Of course, some of the excess can be removed from each end if preferred.

STEERING GEOMETRY

Fork rake is the distance by which the front wheel spindle is offset perpendicular to the steering axis. It is chosen in relation to head angle in order to achieve the desired amount of trail, which is a key variable in cycle geometry as it has a significant influence on the way a bicycle handles.

Trail is the distance by which the front tyre's point of contact with the ground follows the intersection with the ground of the steering axis. It results from the combination of wheel size, head angle and fork rake. Most current road forks used with 700c wheels and a 73° head angle have a rake of between 43mm and 45mm.

If the head angle is made shallower or fork rake is reduced, then trail becomes longer, making the cycle more stable at speed in a straight line and quicker steering when leant over.

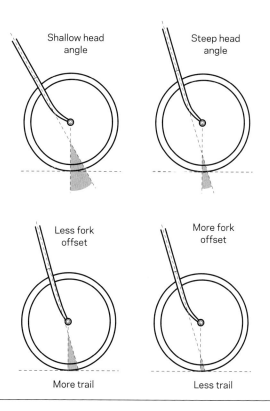

Shallow head angle

Steep head angle

Less fork offset

More fork offset

More trail

Less trail

Brake mounts

Most road bike forks are designed to accept a caliper brake
bolted through the crown, which will be drilled accordingly.
If cantilever or linear-pull brakes are to be used, the blades
will be fitted with mounting bosses, preferably on the front
of the fork for the sake of appearance. A front wheel disc
brake requires a caliper mount at the end of the right-hand
blade, which needs to be much stiffer than a conventional
blade in order to cope with the bending loads imposed as
the caliper pushes against the back of the blade. It's a
problem easily answered with carbon-fibre construction
but requiring a substantially beefed-up blade in a steel fork.

Headset

Largely unloved and routinely ignored, the steering head bearing assembly, or headset, barely receives attention from even the most nit-picking of cycle mechanics unless it goes wrong. It is the component that cyclists forget as far as possible and yet a loose, stiff or notchy headset will spoil the handling of a road bike as surely as a flat tyre.

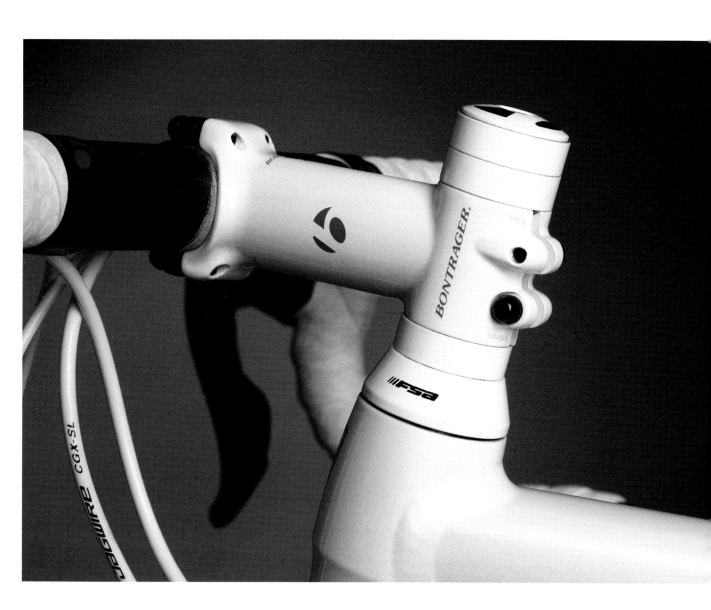

In principle, there isn't much that can go wrong with a headset; a race or seat on the fork crown presses against a lower bearing located in the head tube to hold it into place. The lower bearing transfers rider weight from the frame to the fork crown and road shock from the fork to the frame. Unless shielded by a mudguard, it is exposed to dirt thrown by the front tyre. The lower bearing usually fails before the upper, which keeps the steering column, or steerer, aligned in the head tube and can be moved relative to the tube to provide a means of adjusting bearing play.

Threaded headset

Until the rigours of mountain biking exposed its limitations, the traditional threaded headset was thought to work well. The upper bearing cup moves up or down the steerer on a fine thread and, once adjusted to take up slack, is secured by a lock nut. Widely spaced flats are provided for the spanners used to hold the cup and lock nut. The nut's maximum diameter is kept to a minimum by using eight flats.

As each flat on an octagonal nut is shorter than it would be on the same width hexagonal nut, the spanner can't apply as much torque. The need to minimise stack height – the cumulative thickness of the various components that make up the headset – means the flats are shallow, offering the spanners little purchase. The spanner on the lock nut in particular is apt to slip. Assuming sufficient torque to secure the nut can be applied by a skilled mechanic, the cup will be found to have turned with it, over-tightening the bearing so that the process has to start again.

Other issues associated with the threaded headset include the need to cut the steerer to suit its stack height including washer while ensuring there is enough thread to allow the locknut to bite. Then there's the one that prompted the invention of the threadless headset; if the locknut loosens on the road – or trail – it can't be made secure without two hefty spanners. The only option is to reach down regularly and give the top cup a tightening twist.

Threadless headset

The threadless system not only makes headset adjustment quick and easy using small, lightweight hex keys but provides, in the form of the extended steerer tube, a large diameter, stiff post to which to clamp the stem. Bearing play is taken up by slackening the stem's steerer clamp screws and turning the cap screw to pull the stem against the upper headset cup, otherwise free floating. It slides down the steerer to press the bearings together.

The bearings themselves always use rolling elements, which may be balls or rollers; 'low friction' plastic bushings have been tried but without success, since a freely moving headset is critical to a bike's handling. Close packed and loose balls, once the universal fitment, spilt forth as the headset was pulled apart for re-greasing. Caging the balls cured this but reduced the number of contact points, shortening headset life by making the lower bearing race more susceptible to indenting. Caged rollers enjoyed a spell of popularity in the 1990s and work well if kept lubricated. The difficulty of sealing the gap between the crown race and lower bearing cup is such that this rarely happens.

Separate bearing elements have been replaced in current headsets by sealed cartridge bearings that need no maintenance, last well and are easily replaced when they fail. They are used on external cup and concealed 'integral' head bearing designs. In the latter implementation, the bearings sit directly in profiled seats cut into the head tube.

External bearing cups are press-fitted into the head tube, which must first be reamed to precise dimensions to ensure a secure fit. The internal diameter of a standard 1¼in (31.7mm) head tube, for example, is 29.7mm. To accept an external head bearing with shoulder diameter of 30.2mm, it must be reamed to 30.1mm to provide the required press fit. A fork with oversized 1⅛in (28.6mm) steerer tube requires a 36mm OD head tube, which must be reamed to 33.9mm to accept an oversized 1⅛in external headset bearing cup.

1. Cap bolt
2. Top cap
3. Star nut
4. Top or dust cover
5. Spacers
6. Upper bearing seat with upper bearing and compression ring
7. Lower bearing seat lower bearing
8. Fork crown bearing seat

Suspension

Road bikes don't have suspension as such but make do instead with air-filled tyres. Indeed, so effective are pneumatic tyres at soaking up the minor bumps and holes found in metalled roads that sprung-frame suspension of the type seen on the Lindley and Biggs 'Whippet' (p. 29) disappeared almost as soon as it was introduced.

Absorbing vibration and shock

As road surfaces improved, so tyres could be made narrower and inflated harder in search of reductions in weight and rolling resistance. Frame designs also bolstered suspension.

Frame

Some vibration and shock gets past the air cushion provided by high-pressure tyres and efforts to avoid it are often highly imaginative. They include the suspension seat post, which incorporates a mechanism, often telescopic, that allows the saddle to bob up and down. Suspension handlebar stems, first introduced on mountain bikes, have been tried and discarded. Perhaps the wildest machine to enjoy commercial success was the Allsop Softride, which, like the broadly similar TitanFlex, employed a near

horizontal beam cantilevered back from the head tube to support the saddle. As the beam flexes, so the saddle moves. The layout proved popular with triathletes until banned in 'draft-legal' races by the sport's organising body.

Trek's Domane goes a step further by keeping the seat tube separate from the frame at the junction of the top tube and seatstays, connecting it by means of a bearing pivot that allows the tube to flex below the pivot. This gives the seat some freedom, controlled by the stiffness of the seat tube, to move fore and aft; in practice, there is up to 30mm of vertical movement, sufficient to absorb a significant amount of vibration. Favoured by Paris–Roubaix winner Fabian Cancellara, the IsoSpeed frame is partnered by a fork shaped to deflect more than usual.

▶ RockShox Roubaix
suspension fork.

1. Steerer tube
2. Fork crown
3. Fork stanchion
4. One-piece cast alloy
   lower fork slider

ROCKSHOX PARIS-ROUBAIX FORK

The concept of 'proper' suspension – dependent on separately moving parts – made an appearance in workable form at the Paris-Roubaix classic road race, which is run over a mixture of tarmac roads and pavé, or cobbles. In 1992 and 1993, cyclist Gilbert Duclos-Lassalle of France won the race using the RockShox Roubaix suspension fork, which employed the telescopic action of most motorcycle forks.

For the 1994 race, the Belgian Johan Museeuw turned up with a Bianchi that featured, in addition to a RockShox fork, a rear suspension system based on a swingarm controlled by a coil spring and damper. Plagued by mechanical problems during the race, which was won by Andrei Tchmil of Russia riding a RockShox fork, Museeuw faltered. His failure cast a shadow over full suspension, but even the hat-trick of successes for the suspension fork alone was not enough to sustain the interest of professional racers, who turned back to conventional machines.

Some vibration and shock gets past the air cushion provided by high-pressure tyres. The inherent resilience, or 'springiness', of the many components that transmit road bumps to the hands, feet and seat absorbs much of it. Frames and forks designed to flex more than usual over bumps have proven popular. Curved seatstays, which deflect more than straight stays when subject to compression loads, are increasingly seen on current road bikes such as Cannondale's Synapse, while the Specialized Roubaix features rhomboid openings in the stays designed to flex over bumps and compress the lozenge-shaped Zertz polymer shock absorbers that sit inside them. Similar inserts in the fork blades are designed to do the same at the front end.

Tyres

The process of narrower tyres and increased tyre inflation was seen in the development of the French randonneur touring cycles of the 1920s and '30s. French minor roads of the era were notorious for their poor surfaces and 'balloon' tyres of 50mm or more in width were produced to soak up the worst of the rocks and ruts. Narrower tyres were found to work as well and by the mid-1930s, the width of the most popular tyres had shrunk to as little as 40mm. After the war, cyclists abandoned such fat tyres in favour of the lighter and narrower tyres used by racing cyclists and the 700c format is now practically unchallenged for fast road cycling.

Accessories

Other ways to combat vibration include wrapping the handlebars with extra layers of foam tape, wearing padded gloves, fitting slightly fatter tyres and riding a saddle equipped with damping inserts. Perhaps the final word should go to 1969 Paris–Roubaix winner Walter Godefroot, who scorned the trappings of comfort. Instead, he rode the pavé with one thin layer of cloth handlebar tape and claimed never to have raced wearing gloves or mitts. Enough said.

3

Wheels

The first, and most important, upgrade to make to any road bike is fitting a faster wheelset. Competition road bike wheels are lighter, stiffer and more aerodynamic than ever, but still employ the tension-spoke cycle wheel – one of the most effective uses of material in any sphere of engineering and the same basic technology that has kept cyclists rolling for the last 140 years.

Wheels: A Short History

The bicycle wheel is a highly sophisticated and yet a durable and easily maintained structure. Able to support over 100 times its own weight, stiff and resilient, and suitable for manufacture using low-cost or high-tech materials as required, it is surely the most intricate piece of engineering in a road bike.

▼ Highly tensioned spokes, usually steel, remain the best way to connect the hub and rim of a lightweight cycle wheel.

Early cart wheel

Wheels fitted to the earliest bicycle, the Michaux velocipede or 'boneshaker', were, in essence, cart wheels. The method of construction was proven to work for carts and carriages and there was nothing better available. It presented the early cycle makers with two basic drawbacks: it created a wheel that was, like everything else about the velocipede, both heavy and rigid because the spokes, made of wood, worked in compression; the spoke at the bottom of the wheel where it touched the ground supported the hub and cycle (or cart) weighing down upon it.

Introducing wire spokes

Progress was rapid. The tensioned wire spoke appeared in 1869 in a radical machine called the Phantom. Then in 1871 came the Ariel bicycle introduced by the English cycle engineer James Starley – otherwise known as the father of the bicycle industry.

The Phantom

The 'Phantom' was presumably given its name because, weighing some 24kg (53lb) it was insubstantial compared to its predecessors. Its frame was made of iron rods and was articulated in the middle, but if that wasn't enough, its wheels featured wire spokes held in tension between the rim and the hub flanges so that the rim was suspended from the spokes arrayed around the top half of the wheel.

Pulling inwards on the rim, the spokes could be much thinner and, taken together, lighter than a few wooden spokes in compression. The Phantom's spokes were arranged in pairs, each comprising a single length of wire

passed through a loop in the rim and bent into a 'V' with the ends secured at the hub. Tension was applied to all the spokes at once by forcing the hub flanges apart to increase the distance from rim to flange. Radiating out from the hub to the rim in conventional cart wheel style, the spokes in the bike's driving wheel would have allowed the front hub to twist within the rim when force was applied to the pedals.

The Ariel

The Ariel bicycle improved on the Phantom's method of tensioning the spokes by fitting the front wheel with a bar running across the hub through the middle of the wheel. From the trailing ends of the bar ran adjustable tie-rods, which were attached to the rim. They served to pull it around the hub and thus apply tension to the spokes.

Pulled at a tangent by the hub, the tie rods also ensured there would be no 'wind-up' of the hub under pedalling. Starley followed up this idea by patenting the tangent-spoked wheel in the *annus mirabilis* of 1874, when W. H. J. Grout of Stoke Newington also patented a method of adjusting spoke tension by means of threaded nipples located in the rim. Arguments over the merits of tangent versus radial spokes continued for a decade and radial spoke lacing continued to be used in some ordinary or high-wheel bicycles until their demise.

▶ Both radial and tangential spoke lacing patterns were used with success on the huge wheel of the ordinary or penny-farthing bicycle.

Attaching spokes to wheel rims

By 1895, when the ordinary bicycle had all but disappeared, the radial spoke pattern had been abandoned in favour of J-bend tangent spokes located in flanged hubs with nipples at the rim. The cycle wheel had arrived at something approaching its classic form, although rim technology still offered plenty of scope for experiment and improvement.

Cycle tyres were, as now, essentially of two types: one-piece tubular tyres stuck to the rim were favoured for racing while wired-on tyres that allowed ready access to the inner tube were the choice for leisure. Wired-on tyre rims were made of pressed and rolled steel sheet or, in the case of some luxury machines, aluminium strip. By the early 1970s, aluminium wired-on rims were a common fitment on sports roadsters but employed a weak, flexible single-wall profile.

Wooden rims

For a several decades, the finest racing cycles rolled on wooden rims wearing tubular tyres. Wood proved a material well suited to the application; spoke tension pulls the rim inwards, putting it in compression. Wood's low density means a wooden rim can have the large cross-sectional area needed in a compression member, allowing the wheel to be built with greater spoke tension and therefore fewer spokes than is possible in a wheel with the necessarily thin folded strip of a reasonably light steel rim. It is also easy to shape to the cross section required for a glued-on tubular tyre.

▼ Wooden cycle rims, superseded by hollow aluminium models in the 1930s, are still made today and offer a distinctive riding experience.

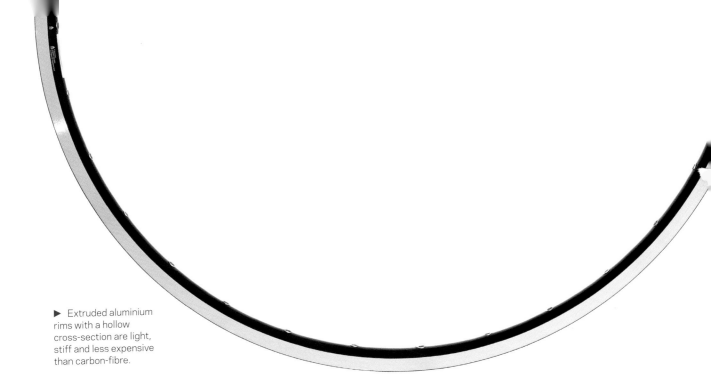

▶ Extruded aluminium rims with a hollow cross-section are light, stiff and less expensive than carbon-fibre.

Aluminium rims

For the 1934 Tour de France, the ever innovative French firm Mavic supplied leading professional road racer Antonin Magne with double-wall or box-section hollow aluminium rims of a revolutionary new design featuring pressed-steel reinforcing eyelets let into the rim. Each eyelet comprised a top-hat shape stamped out of sheet steel with a nipple-sized hole in the crown. The eyelet sat in a hole in the rim outer wall the same diameter as its sleeve section with the brim resting against the outer wall and the face of the crown resting against the inside in the inner wall. Thus the brim and crown shared the pull of the spoke nipple between the rim's inner and outer walls. Without the eyelet, the inner, hub-side wall of the rim's box section needed to be thick and therefore heavy to resist the pull of the spoke.

As such novelties were forbidden by the race rules, the rims were painted to look like wood to avoid detection. Although comparable in weight with wooden racing rims, they proved much stiffer and gave Magne a huge competitive advantage that he used to win the Tour in convincing style, beating his nearest challenger by over 27 minutes and recording an average speed of more than 31kph (19.3mph) for the first time in the event's history.

Amazingly, this major advance over previous attempts to make light but durable aluminium rims was developed simultaneously by Mavic and an Italian designer Mario Longhi, who filed his patent two hours before Mavic, but thereafter allowed the French firm to manufacture eyelets rims until the patent expired in 1947. In order to avoid infringing on the Mavic-Longhi patent, rivals tried alternative methods of stiffening the hollow rim, such as sandwiching a wooden strip inside it.

The double-eyeletted rim proved the best design and Mavic improved it still further with a patent registered in 1966. The eyelet was fixed firmly to the inner rim wall by crimping a small tubular protrusion pushed through the spoke hole. This is the method of anchoring the spoke nipple still widely used today for both tubular and clincher rims with a hollow-box cross section. Some lightweight aluminium rims omit the eyelet and rely on a roughly delta-shaped profile, with the nipple at its tip, to resist spoke tension.

The hollow box section of the tubular or 'sprint' rim makes for a very light structure but was not found on rims suitable for wired-on tyres until the arrival of the Mavic Module E rim (see pp. 60–61) and Michelin's matching Elan tyre. Together, they immediately improved the performance of the wired-on or clincher tyre to the point where it was comparable to that of a heavy duty training tubular and, as clincher performance steadily improved, to that of even the fastest of road-racing tubs.

'Factory-built' rims

Recent developments in wheel manufacturing have centred on perfecting the 'factory-built' wheelset, which has largely replaced the handbuilt wheel for all but touring and audax riding, and on finding improvements in wheel aerodynamics. Rims designed using computational fluid dynamics (CFD) and manufactured in carbon-fibre demonstrate a marked reduction in air drag but can weigh as little as a box-section aluminium sprint rim. Their cost is high and the challenge for the industry is to make such speedy wheels available to all road cyclists.

Wheel Tension

Bicycle wheels need to be light, strong, as close to perfectly round as possible and, for the road, resilient. Their structure relies on a web of thin, highly tensioned spokes to hold the hub within the rim, which is held in compression along its circumference by spoke tension.

▶ L–R: Chrome-plated brass nipple, spoke thread, J-bend spoke head.

Construction

Small changes in spoke tension alter the pull on the wheel rim axially, or sideways, and radially, or inwards towards the hub, and permit a skilled builder to true the rim to a tolerance of less than half a millimetre in either plane.

One end of the spoke has a thread to permit tension adjustment; the other may also be threaded and anchored either directly in the hub or, as with the German manufacturer Cytech's design, in small inserts that are themselves screwed into the hub. Steel spokes will almost always have a mushroom head, which in a classic J-bend spoke sits just beyond the bend. The length of this section should correspond with the thickness of the hub flange. If the flange is too thin, the spoke bend will sit some way out from the flange and allow the spoke to flex during riding leading to early fatigue. The solution is to install a brass washer under the head of the spoke before lacing. The washer must go between the spoke head and flange, not between the flange and bend.

Once the wheel has been laced (see p. 57) and tension put into the spokes, they should be stressed by squeezing together adjacent spokes and then pressing them against the sides of the flanges to remove any residual curvature, caused by the fit of the J-bend in the flange, as it will lead to flex. Straight-pull spokes have an easier time, since there is no bend that can be flexed. Even so, the use of straight-pull spokes is no guarantee against failure as any misalignment of the spoke shaft between hub and rim can lead to fatigue.

WHEEL LACING

Spokes can be laced in a variety of unusual patterns, some of which are of little practical purpose. One exception is the 'crow's foot' arrangement, which uses one radial spoke sitting between two crossing spokes. The pattern is supposed to combine excellent lateral stiffness and efficient drive and is seen today in the DT Swiss Tricon wheel.

The most commonly used lacing patterns are simple and leave the spokes running radially, in which case they do not cross, or crossing one, two or three other spokes on the same side of the wheel. Spokes can be radial on one side and crossing, or tangent, on the other.

Tangent spoking, used to transmit torque between hub and rim, may only be needed on one side of the wheel and is typically seen in rear wheels. It is also needed in a front wheel with a disc or drum brake. Four-cross lacing is occasionally used but adds weight while offering no advantage over three-cross.

It is often argued that tangent-spoked wheels are 'softer' and more comfortable than those with radial spokes, but any difference in vertical flexibility and hence bump absorption is negligible. The spokes of a conventional handbuilt wheel are usually built three-cross on both sides of the front and rear wheels for looks and convenience and to avoid stressing hub flanges that aren't designed for radial lacing.

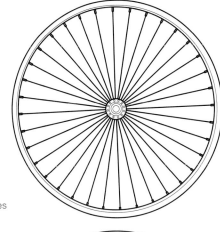

▶ Radial spokes

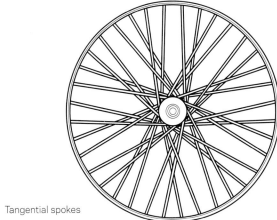

▶ Tangential spokes

Material tension

Besides steel, tension spokes can be made of aluminium, titanium or carbon-fibre. Composites offer possibilities that were first realised by German firm Lightweight. Their famously light wheels use composite spokes kept under tension during the building process and incorporated as part of the final one-piece wheel moulding. The wheels are non-adjustable, but the stiffness of the carbon-fibre rim is such that the wheels do not go out of true unless broken.

Wheel science

A wire spoke is able to support a load in tension many times greater than in compression and is unable to resist much compression without buckling. A 300mm Sapim Race spoke will support over 2600N in tension but will buckle under about 12N. Only a few spokes in tension are needed to support the weight of bike and rider. The second version of Campagnolo's Shamal wheelset used just 12 spokes per wheel.

A 700c wheel with a low spoke count needs a rigid rim, since the spokes are widely spaced. The first factory-built performance wheelset was Mavic's Helium design, which was intended for use by climbers. Its lightweight construction proved fragile and the generation of wheels that followed, typified by Campagnolo's original 16-spoke Shamal, employed strong, rigid but heavy rims in order to improve durability and thus reduce the manufacturer's exposure to warranty claims.

The heavy duty but rigid rim formula works well but at the expense of overall wheel weight. Efforts to lose it have resulted in wheels with a light rim and relatively few spokes under very high tension. Should a spoke break, the rim is immediately pulled a long way out of true and may require a complete rebuild. In this respect, traditional handbuilt wheels offer superior usability for similar overall weight. They usually employ a shallow, light and relatively flexible rim and a high spoke count, which lessens the workload of each and makes rim re-truing easier when needed.

▼ Wheels with as few as 12 tensioned spokes have proven strong enough for competitive cycling and save on both weight and wind resistance.

Rear wheels

Rear wheels for derailleur gears are 'dished' to provide space in the hub for the sprocket cassette. As the right-hand flange sits closer to the hub centre, its spokes leave the hub at a shallower angle and exert less of a sideways pull on the rim. The drive-side spokes are, therefore, at higher tension than the non-drive.

This is more of a problem for the non-drive side spokes, which may not have enough tension to stay tight over bumps. One solution is to use an asymmetric rim profile, which offsets all spokes to the non-drive side of the rim; the other is to use fewer non-drive spokes, usually half the number on the drive side, so that each does more work and needs greater tension.

Factory-built rear wheels with a low spoke count are often laced one- or two-cross on one side only and radially on the other. Radial spokes (see p. 57), which take the shortest distance between hub and rim, build into a wheel that is light and laterally stiff but does not transmit drive torque effectively as the hub can 'wind up' relative to the rim. All-radial spoking is therefore best confined to front wheels for use with rim brakes.

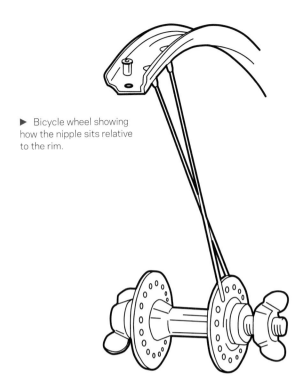

▶ Bicycle wheel showing how the nipple sits relative to the rim.

▼ Pressed-steel eyelets transmit the pull of the spokes to the rim.

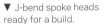

▼ J-bend spoke heads ready for a build.

Rims: Types

The modern road bike's rim design and construction date from the development in the 1930s of reliable and sturdy box-section aluminium rims for tubular tyres. The rims used for wired-on tyres stuck with the inferior single-wall cross section for over 40 years, merely going through a series of minor changes introduced to accommodate improvements in braking and materials technology.

▲ Mavic Open Pro rim

Form

Suitable for use with rod-operated pull-up brakes, the Westwood rim was by the 1930s discarded for performance cycle use in favour of the Endrick design. Originally made by rolling thin steel sheet into a profile that incorporated small hollow spaces at the sides, the Endrick featured tall sidewalls that provided tracks for brake blocks. Braking performance may have been no better but wheel removal was made much easier.

By the 1950s Endrick-pattern rims in aluminium were widely available. Since the extra material thickness made possible by the metal's light weight improved the stiffness of the rim and aluminium provided a better braking surface for rubber blocks, aluminium Endrick rims were the preferred option for sports riding until rendered obsolete by Mavic's Module E in 1975.

Featuring a double-wall box section based on that of a tubular tyre rim, the Module E set the pattern for the high-performance clincher rims that followed over the next 20 years. From the mid-1990s onwards, both clincher and tubular rims benefitted from efforts to improve wheel aerodynamics and the increasing use of carbon-fibre construction. Advances in the two have been closely interlinked, since the rim profiles that generate the least aerodynamic drag also require the most material.

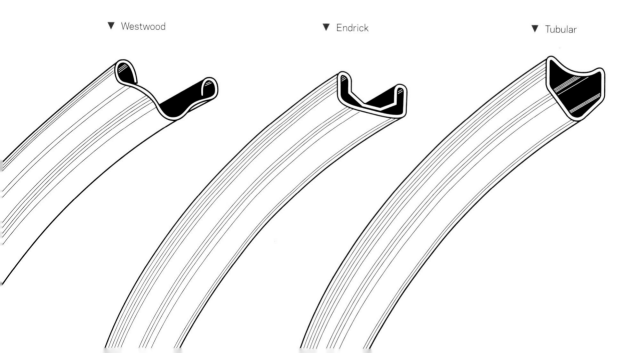

▼ Westwood ▼ Endrick ▼ Tubular

▶ Bontrager's Aeolus 5 wheelset features deep-section moulded carbon-fibre rims with an aerodynamically efficient profile.

Material

Aluminium rims shaped to reduce air drag made by Assos, Switzerland and Araya, Japan appeared in the early 1980s and were quickly followed by deeper, more effective shapes realised in carbon-fibre such as those made by Steve Hed. The next generation of 'aero' wheels was headed by Campagnolo's original Shamal, which heralded the big manufacturers' growing interest in making faster road bike wheels. Previously, interest in wheel aerodynamics had been the preserve of triathletes and time triallists. The Shamal brought the 'aero' wheelset to the road.

Its all-aluminium rims were very heavy, however, and moulded carbon-fibre was clearly a superior material for making deep-section rims. Following the path beaten by HED and Zipp, larger manufacturers turned to carbon-fibre and began offering rims in a bewildering variety of profiles, some of which were entirely ineffective at reducing air drag.

Most were made for tubular tyres, since the curved tyre bed proved easy to mould. Clincher convenience could be provided by bonding to the aero carbon-fibre an aluminium sub-rim bearing the required hook bead profile, along with brake tracks. While adding weight, this arrangement has the advantage of providing the consistent braking performance lacking with most all-carbon rims and remains popular on lower-priced aero rims.

Mavic's Cosmic Carbone design took a different route by wrapping a teardrop-shaped carbon-fibre cladding around the hub side of the rim to create an affordable, very popular and highly influential wheelset. It nevertheless proved something of a cul-de-sac in wheel development, for the next and most recent generation of wheels went back to all-carbon construction for both tubular and clincher rims.

More importantly, the rim profiles of wheelsets such as Zipp's Firecrest and Bontrager's Aeolus D3 have been developed using computational fluid dynamics (CFD), which has given engineers previously unimagined insights into airflow. The resulting rim profiles all differ in small details as each manufacturer looks for a 'proprietary' shape and their comparative performance is, naturally, hotly contested but all outperform pre-CFD wheels by a huge margin.

An idea of the lengths to which designers are now prepared to go may be gained from Mavic's CXR80. Soft foam Frisbee-like circular 'blades' clip onto the rim on either side of the tyre sidewall to fill in the indent at that point and fair the sides of the tyre into the rim. The blades are banned for professional bike racing but otherwise offer the road cyclist an even sharper aero 'edge'.

Tyres: A Short History

Scottish inventor John Boyd Dunlop created the pneumatic tyre in 1888 and, with it, made possible the bicycle and road transport as we know it today. However, Dunlop was not the first to patent the idea of a tyre containing an inner tube filled with pressurised air; his fellow Scot, Robert William Thomson, got there first in 1845 with his 'Aerial Wheel'. Intended for fitment to horse-drawn coaches, Thomson's tyre comprised multiple inflated tubes inside a flexible covering.

Invention of the pneumatic tyre

Thomson was obliged to abandon his tyre, although it
significantly improved the comfort of the coaches to which
it was fitted, as he was unable to obtain enough of the thin
rubber required for the inner tubes. The existence of his
prior patent, of which Dunlop knew nothing when
developing his own idea, had a profound effect on the
course of pneumatic tyre development in the years
following its application to the fledgling safety bicycle.

Dunlop's tyre, which he invented to improve the ride of his
son's tricycle, proved not only far more comfortable than
solid rubber tyres but very much easier to propel. It
transformed the safety bicycle, previously a sluggish and
wretchedly uncomfortable alternative to the high-wheeled
ordinary bicycle, into a machine that was not only less
hazardous but significantly faster and, by 1895, both the
ordinary bicycle and solid tyres were entirely obsolete.

The pneumatic tyre's victory was complete, but, sadly for
Dunlop, who began manufacturing tyres in Ireland, the
prior existence of the Thomson tyre meant that his patent
was declared invalid within two years of being granted.
Suddenly, anyone could manufacture and sell an air-filled
tyre. The subsequent free-for-all produced a flood of
innovation as inventors attempted to overcome the new
tyre's one major drawback: not so much the puncture itself
but the difficulty of mending one.

Puncture repair

Early adopters rode pneumatics stuck directly to the rim
and presumably accepted the inconvenience of having to
remove and refit the tyre to get at the inner tube but, for
the pneumatic tyre to be truly useful to the cyclist travelling
on the road, puncture repair had to be quick, if not
necessarily easy. Proof of the advantage to be gained from
a rapid means of repair was supplied by Michelin. The
French firm began making cycle tyres in 1891 and Charles
Terront rode Michelins on his winning ride in the inaugural
race from Paris to Brest and back in 1891. The tyre cover
was secured to the rim by means of steel bands tightened
on to it by screws, which could be removed to pull the
cover away from the rim for access to the tube.

In 1892, Michelin not only organised a race from Paris to
the company's home city of Clermont-Ferrand but had
nails strewn across the road. History does not relate the
response of those competitors not riding Michelin rubber.

Wire beading

Ingenious though it was, the Michelin and other similar
concepts had already been rendered obsolete by a wire-
bead tyre patented in 1890 by Englishman Charles Welch.
His idea proved to be by far the most effective way to
attach a quickly detachable pneumatic tyre to a rim and
features in virtually every motor vehicle tyre made today. It
comprises the rim flanges, the trough or well between them
and an endless wire bead running around each edge of the
cover. The flange, trough and bead are concentric when the
tyre is inflated. Because the flange outer circumference is
greater than the bead circumference, there is only one way
to get the bead over the flange without stretching it by
force. The bead on one half of the wheel drops into the
trough, making available enough slack in the bead on the
side diametrically opposite to pass over the flange. The
deeper the trough, the more easily the bead will pass over
the flange and the easier the tyre is to fit and remove.
Realising the value of the Welch patent, Dunlop bought it.

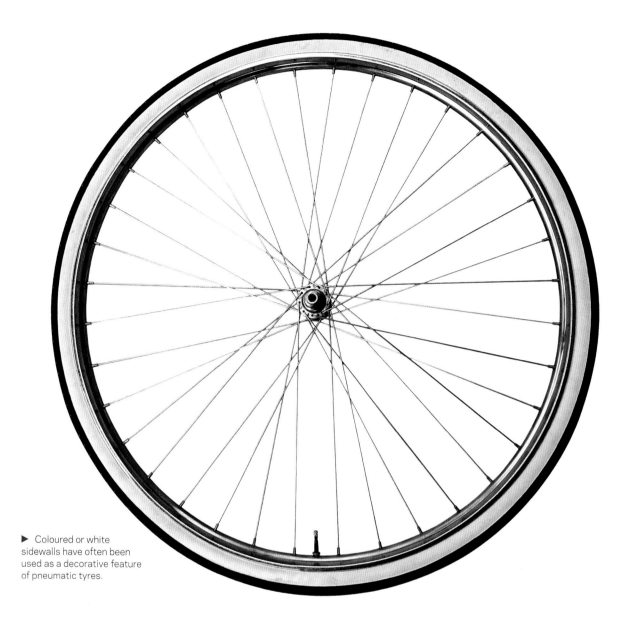

► Coloured or white sidewalls have often been used as a decorative feature of pneumatic tyres.

Clincher tyres

The first detachable pneumatic to reach the cycling market was patented by Englishman William Bartlett a month after Welch's patent: the clincher. Unlike the Welch tyre, it did not employ endless wire beads to hold the tyre cover to the rim. Instead, the edges of the cover featured wedge-shaped beads moulded into the fabric that hooked under a matching profile formed on the insides of the rim. Air pressure alone kept the beads tucked under the rim sides; when pressure was removed, either bead could be pushed away from the rim and pulled over it to get to the tube.

The Dunlop Pneumatic Tyre Co. bought the Bartlett Clincher patent in 1897, thus securing a firm hold on the pneumatic tyre market. The clincher tyre remained a popular fitment on motor cars until entirely superseded by the wired-on type in the 1920s.

Tubular tyres

Cord plies, introduced by American J. F. Palmer in 1892, improved on the woven canvas previously employed for the carcass. Each of the plies was made up of unidirectional cords held together in a coating of rubber gum. Two or more plies were overlaid to create a layered cross-ply structure that separated the constituent fibres to keep them from rubbing against each other.

Thus, the modern pneumatic tyre was born. In one respect, tyre technology has progressed no further. As enduring as the coelacanth, the one-piece 'tubular' tyre stuck to the rim is still the first choice for top level competition on the road.

That 'tubs', with their archaic attachment to the rim, are still being used after 120 years of technological innovation in the detachable tyre might seem perverse, but the demands of competition don't include ease of access to the inner tube. Since a tube can be ripped from the rim and a spare fitted and inflated long before a skilled mechanic can remove one inner tube, fit a replacement and fit the cover, tubs make more sense than clinchers in terms of quickly getting back into action after a flat.

More important to professional racers is that a tub can be ridden in reasonable safety when flat. A punctured clincher tyre is likely to come away from the rim, either wrapping itself around and locking the wheel or leaving the rim in contact with the ground and with no grip. Glued firmly to the rim, a punctured tub allows the rider to keep going until a team car arrives with a spare wheel.

Design development

For decades following the demise of the original Bartlett Clincher, the Welch Dunlop was the only detachable tyre type available. The finest examples were fast enough for touring and general purpose road cycling but, heavy and unable to hold air pressure of much more than 70psi or 5 bar (atmospheres), were no match for even the heaviest of tubular tyres.

The status quo was upended with the introduction in 1975 of the Michelin Elan. It was developed by the tyre manufacturer in association with Mavic and could be fitted only to the fellow French firm's Module E rim. The importance of the tyre and rim pairing is summed up by Mavic's own sales figures. In 1978, clincher tyre rims made up 5% of Mavic's production; within five years the ratio was reversed, with clincher rims making up 95% rim manufacturing output.

Several factors contributed to the success of the combo: of the two rim diameters offered, one was the same as that of the standard tubular tyre rim, so racing cyclists could swap from sprints to clinchers without the need to adjust brake blocks; the Elan tyre was narrow and, therefore, light; and it could be inflated to pressures greatly in excess of those possible with the older wired-on tyres. In 1978, Michelin followed up the Elan with the BIB TS, which had a folding bead of Kevlar fibre; the modern clincher tyre, which equips almost every performance cycle sold today, had arrived.

▲ Removed from the rim, a folding clincher cycle tyre is a shapeless strip of rubber and fabric.

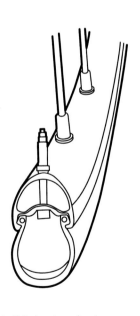

▲ Tubeless tyre showing separate valve

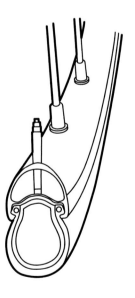

▲ Conventional tyre with inner tube

Tyres: Construction

The pneumatic tyre comprises a tread laid over a carcass equipped with a means of attachment to the rim. The tread provides adhesion with the road surface and acts as the first line of defence against puncture. Its compound may be a mixture of natural and butyl rubbers and contains a filler material that strengthens the rubber and modifies the way its molecules interact, improving grip and rolling resistance. Finely ground carbon or soot is traditionally used as the filler, but alternatives including clay and silica allow the compound to be coloured rather than black.

Carcass

The carcass gives the tyre its shape and resists the pressure exerted by the air inside. That of a conventional cycle tyre has the plies overlaid at 90° to each other and, therefore, at 45° to the wheel's direction of rotation in a conventional cross-ply layout. Each ply is composed of one row of close-packed fibre cords or threads held together by rubber; the more slender each thread, the greater the number that can be packed into a section of ply and the higher the thread count. A carcass with a higher Threads Per Inch (tpi) figure is thinner and therefore lighter, more flexible and, in principle, faster. Most road bike tyres feature an additional breaker ply placed under the thread to improve puncture resistance, which may be enhanced by a woven belt of Kevlar or Vectran fibre.

Uniquely, Vittoria's Diamante Pro Radiale has a 'radial' carcass, in which the plies are laid at 85° to the direction of rotation and, therefore, at 10° to each other. With less interference between the plies, the tyre carcass can deform more readily. Vittoria claims an improvement in comfort and rolling resistance but, in practice, the tyre must be inflated to a higher pressure than a cross-ply to avoid imprecise handling characteristics, thus negating any possible advantage.

1. Tread
2. Puncture protection rubber belt
3. Reflex strip
4. Rubber sidewall
5. Twisted steel wire
6. Bicycle tyre carcass

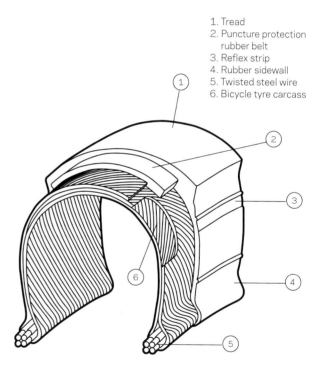

Tyre pressure

Pneumatic tyres should be inflated to a pressure that suits the rider; too soft a tyre impairs handling, slows the cycle and increases the risk of puncture while too high a pressure reduces grip and generates a harsh ride. Trial and error is an effective method for finding the optimal pressure. Many tyres now have minimum and maximum pressure markings moulded into the sidewall. The maximum must not be exceeded to avoid the risk of tyre blow-off.

Tubular tyres

Tubular tyres (see pp. 64–65) are glued to the rim using either cement or an adhesive tape. The tyre's base tape covers the stitching that holds the edges of the tub carcass together with the inner tube inside. This 'one-piece' construction allows the tub to hold immense air pressure without stressing the rim; track racers may inflate their tubular tyres to 200psi or more. On the road, pressures of around 95psi work best, allowing the tyre to roll easily over rough surfaces.

Clincher tyres

The modern clincher cannot reliably withstand pressures of more than 160psi but will retain pressures higher than those possible with older wired-on tyres. It combines the important features of the Welch and old style clincher designs (see pp. 64–65). The tyre has either wire or foldable Kevlar bead loops and the bead profile's lip engages with a hook on the rim flange.

The design means that both the bead and the hook interface contribute to holding the tyre on the rim. That the hook profile shares the work can be demonstrated by severing the wire or foldable bead loop in one or more places so that it cannot hold the tyre in place. After carefully installing the lip of the bead under the rim hook, the tyre can be inflated to 100psi or more without blowing off the rim. It must not be ridden in this condition. The hook and bead arrangement holds more than the recommended pressure but under extreme air pressure will stretch enough to allow the tyre to blow off the rim. The maximum pressure a clincher will withstand is higher than that marked on the sidewall.

TYRE VALVES

Road bikes use the Presta tyre valve in preference to the Schrader valve found in most pneumatic tyres. 2mm smaller in diameter, the Presta valve minimises the size of the valve hole in a narrow road bike rim. The small nut on the threaded toggle must be tightened after inflation to prevent accidental deflation. The stem itself is vulnerable to damage and care must be taken not to bend it. Latex inner tubes are sometimes used in preference to heavier butyl but lose air more quickly and are more fragile.

Tyres: Performance

One of the most hotly debated aspects of road bike technology is the question of whether tubular tyres are better than clinchers. In practice, the debate centres on speed and comfort, with tubular aficionados stoutly maintaining that 'tubs' score highly on both.

Puncture

There is one area where tubular tyres unquestionably outperform clinchers on the road. Whereas a clincher, once punctured, is highly likely to come off the rim, a flatted tub will stay in place, glued to the rim. This is the primary reason that 'tubs' are still favoured for racing by professionals and the best example of the benefit to be had is arguably that provided by Spaniard Abraham Olano. Olano won the 1995 World Road Race Championships in Colombia with a lone break on the last lap from a group that included his team mate Miguel Indurain. Olano punctured with about 4km remaining. Although his rear wheel could be seen moving around on the tyre, he retained enough control to be able to keep riding to the finish for the win.

Braking

Braking from high speed puts a lot of heat into a cycle wheel rim. On a long descent, this can raise the temperature of the air inside a clincher, increasing its pressure and blowing the tyre off the rim. Or, it can soften the cement or glue holding a tubular tyre to the rim; in the worst case, the tyre may creep around the rim or even roll upside down, leaving the cyclist riding on the base tape. Here, honours are about even.

▼ Brightly coloured tyre treads rely on the use of silica or clay as a rubber filler in place of carbon particles.

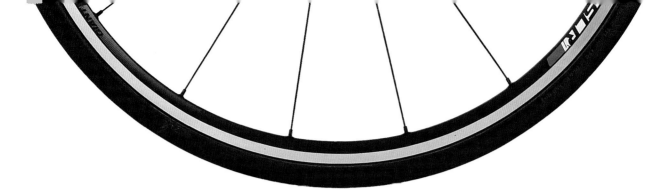

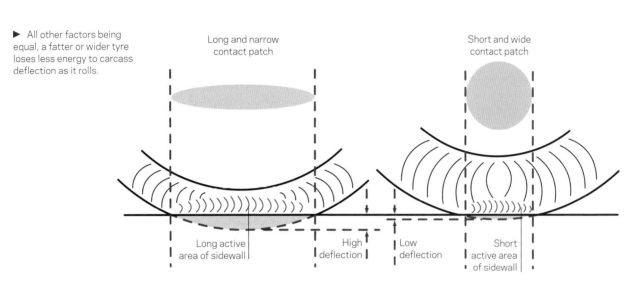

▶ All other factors being equal, a fatter or wider tyre loses less energy to carcass deflection as it rolls.

Long and narrow contact patch

Short and wide contact patch

Long active area of sidewall

High deflection

Low deflection

Short active area of sidewall

Pinch flat

Many proponents argue that 'tubs' are less likely to suffer a 'pinch' flat when rolling over a sharp edge. When this happens, the inner tube gets caught between the rim and the edge of, for example, a hole, usually leaving two and occasionally four telltale holes in a 'snakebite' pattern. The rounded edges of the tubular rim are considered to pose less of a risk to the tube than do the raised sides of the clincher design.

Ride comfort

Superior ride comfort is also claimed for the tubular when fitted to a classic box-section sprint rim. Again, the culprit is held to be the clincher rim's raised sides, which make the rim deeper and less easily deflected in the radial plane. The use of rigid deep-section rims of either format renders this argument null. Although the combined weight of a clincher tyre, inner tube and base tape is usually within a few grammes of that of a comparable tub, the clincher rim is, inevitably, heavier. This is especially true of older deep-section clincher rims fitted with an aluminium sub-rim to hold the tyre.

Rolling resistance

At the root of the tubular versus clincher debate, however, is the question of rolling resistance. According to their advocates, 'tubs' roll faster. It's a difficult question to resolve, since there are so many variables involved. Tyre width, tread depth, carcass quality, inflation pressure, inner tube thickness, whether the inner tube is made of butyl, rubber or latex and even the type of base tape fitted to a clincher rim may affect the outcome. It is hard to find directly comparable clincher and tubular tyres, where tread depth, pattern and compound, carcass construction and tyre width are the same.

The best evidence suggests that a road clincher rolls slightly faster than a directly comparable tubular and the reason is that the cement, tape or glue holding the tub to the rim is soft and compressible but not very elastic. It allows the tub to flatten against the rim at the point passing over the ground but slows its return, so some of the energy absorbed as the tyre compresses is lost to slow recovery.

Any difference is small and outweighed by the many other considerations. Ultimately, the convenience and ease of repair offered by clinchers makes them the more popular choice. The debate will surely widen to include tubeless tyre technology as it improves and becomes more widely accepted.

Spokes

By far the most widely used material for bicycle spokes is stainless steel. The reliable and fatigue resistant stainless steel spokes that became available from the early 1980s onwards quickly replaced both the 'rustless' steel spokes used for less expensive road bikes and the chrome-plated high-tensile steel spokes preferred for high-end cycles. While they looked great when freshly polished, chromed spokes were prone to breakage and needed frequent cleaning to prevent the rapid onset of rust. Today's stainless steel spokes are superior in both respects.

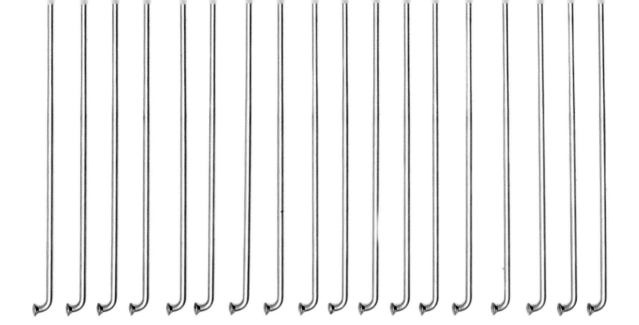

Straight versus J-bend

Spoke breakage is much less of a problem than it once was, thanks in part to improvements in metallurgy and cold-forging production techniques, which give the highest quality spokes exceptional fatigue resistance. Factory-built wheelsets have played their part as manufacturers have looked for ways to improve the durability of the product. The straight-pull spokes in widespread use need less care with pre-stressing during the early build process and, if used in a correctly designed wheel, avoid a potential source of the flex that eventually causes fatigue.

Traditional J-bend spokes, which are used with conventional hub flanges, remain popular with small scale wheelbuilders and, if laced and tensioned with care, remain the best option for all-round use as they allow the builder to achieve perfect spoke alignment between the hub flange and rim.

Durability

The leading manufacturers, which include DT Swiss and Sapim, market a potentially bewildering variety of spokes. Sapim's range, for example, includes six butted and two aero models, each of them available in straight-pull or J-bend format and with a choice of colour finish. Stainless steel spokes can be given a black oxidised coating as an alternative to their natural finish.

Double-butted spokes are thinner in the middle than at the ends. A single-butted spoke is thicker at the hub end. Butting adds strength at the head and thread, and saves weight elsewhere. The slender middle section is easily strong enough to resist tension alone; Sapim's race spoke, for example, can support more than 400kg.

Butting also makes a wheel more resilient and more robust. As the spoke is tightened during the build, it is stretched – by more than 1mm in a well-tensioned wheel. A butted spoke stretches more under the same tension than a plain-gauge spoke and so, when a bump in the road presses the rim inwards at that point, can relax further before losing all tension. A wheel built with double-butted spokes will, therefore, stay in true over much rougher terrain.

'Aero' spokes, introduced in the early 1980s, feature an elongated cross section that slices through the air more cleanly than a round spoke. The most effective aero spokes have an elliptical shape; others are simply given flattened sides to reduce their width.

Materials

Alternatives to steel include aluminium and titanium, which enjoyed a brief period of popularity in the mid-1990s. It proved too costly and insufficiently stiff to challenge the performance of stainless steel. Reliable aluminium spokes made their first appearance in Mavic's Ksyrium wheel of 1999 and have been widely used since. Unfortunately, aluminium is only one third as stiff as steel and about one third of the weight, so an aluminium spoke as stiff as a steel one must have a cross section three times greater and weigh about the same. Since a fatter spoke presents a greater frontal area to the wind, the benefits of using aluminium spokes are hard to discern, especially as care must be taken with hub and rim design to avoid potential crack-starters such as threads and bends.

Flexible fibre spokes are used in wheels such as Spinergy's Xaero Lite but are considered to build into a comfortable but soft wheel. The opposite is true of carbon-fibre, which is increasingly used in very high-end wheels, where its rigidity and light weight help achieve exceptional performance. The all-carbon-fibre Reynolds RZR rear wheel's spokes all have an aero profile and only four tangent spokes are needed; they are so stiff that power transfer is immediate.

Nipples

A quick glance at the wheels that equip the majority of road bikes sold today will show that the classic spoke nipple is alive and well. The concept was invented by W. H. J. Grout, who came up with the idea of using wire spokes tensioned individually to keep the wheel rim in true. The conventional nipple is simply a long, slender, four-sided nut threaded over the end of the spoke and provided with a flange that bears inwards against the rim as the spoke is tightened.

▲ The threaded spoke nipple is a convenient means of applying tension to the spoke and transmitting it to the rim.

Rim location

Tradition puts the nipples at the rim, perhaps because that is where Grout found it convenient to locate them. The disadvantage of this arrangement is twofold: the nipple is heavier than a mushroom spoke head, putting weight where it is not wanted, and the nipple's body is thicker than the spoke, thus needing a larger diameter hole that makes the rim weaker. On the other hand, it may be more intuitive to work on nipples at the rim, where the effect of altering tension is seen, and it is easier to make a hub with flanges for the spoke heads than for the nipples.

Shimano's experiment

Both considerations have influenced the evolution of the road wheels made by Shimano. The Japanese manufacturer entered the ready-built wheel market in 1999 with the WH7700 wheelset, a radical design that put the nipples at the hub in studs spaced around it. The spokes crossed from one side of the hub to the opposite side of the rim. Many wheel builders found the layout, which was completely different from anything seen previously, confusing and it was dropped in favour of a more conventional lacing pattern, but the nipples stayed at the hub.

The new wheel had straight-pull spokes with the head inside the rim. Their high tension meant that Shimano had to strengthen the thin wall of the rim with a seat to prevent the small-diameter head from pulling through, thus negating any rotating weight advantage gained by moving the nipples to the hub. They returned to the rim for Shimano's most recent wheel design and look likely to stay there.

Torque

Weight can be saved by using aluminium nipples instead of the usual brass. More expensive and less robust, regular aluminium nipples require care during the build as the flats are prone to round off as they are turned. This can be avoided by using splined nipples, which require a special key but can be torqued to a very high tension.

The nipples of deep-section aero rims are often hidden inside to avoid any interruption of airflow. The nipple must then be provided with an alternative means of applying torque such as a small hex head on the outside end. This, in turn, requires a special T-bar type key since the nipple is always found inside a deep recess.

Many old-school wheel builders eschew any kind of thread-locking compound or 'spoke prep' on the nipple thread as the spokes of a well-tensioned conventional wheel should not need it. However, locking the nipple temporarily to the spoke will prevent it loosening if tension is lost as the rim compresses inwards over a bump and many factory-built wheels employ some means of securing the nipple. The alternative to spoke prep is to equip the nipple with a nylon ring set into the head that grips the thread firmly, allowing the nipple to be turned with a key but preventing movement otherwise.

To avoid cutting a thread in their delicate aluminium spokes, the nipples on Mavic's Ksyrium wheels have the thread on the outside and screw directly into a female thread formed in the rim wall. When tightened, the rim-side face of the nipple pushes against the mushroomed end of the spoke, pushing it away from the hub and thereby applying tension.

◄ Mavic's Ksyrium wheelset uses spokes with nipples that screw into a thread formed in the rim.

Hubs

On the side of the packaging of older Campagnolo hubs and other components containing ball bearings is printed the reassuring information that the balls are selected to a *toleranza di un millesimo*, or a tolerance of one micron. The finer the tolerance, the more smoothly the bearings run, and for a long time Campagnolo made the smoothest running hubs in cycling.

Types

The clean, spare but elegant lines of the classic Campagnolo Record large-flange hub of the late 20th century still win admirers today, but design and technology have moved on. Smooth running bearings are the norm although usually found in the form of annular 'cartridge' bearings pressed into the hub instead of the cup-and-cone bearings once almost the universal fitment for cycle wheels.

On the other hand, the large or 'high' hub flange, which all but disappeared from the market for a couple of decades, is enjoying something of a renaissance thanks to the efforts of manufacturers such as Rolf Prima and American Classic to find ways to bolster wheel stiffness. The large flange does this by shortening the length of the spokes, which are less rigid than the flange, by increasing the pulling-arm radius of tangent spokes and by increasing the sideways pulling angle of the spokes to the rim. As none of these is relevant to front wheel construction, the large flange is now usually found in the rear wheel.

Historically, large flange hubs were used for both front and rear wheels to reduce spoke flex and therefore the likelihood of spoke breakage. Improvements in spoke manufacturing technology have made such considerations redundant and they are now one way to reduce spoke count without compromising on performance.

Large versus small

Flange size varies widely and there is no strict point at which a flange becomes classified as 'large'. The next size down is usually known as a mid-flange and some specialist hub manufacturers will combine a mid-flange on the rear hub drive side with a small flange in order to even out to a degree the spoke tension in a dished rear wheel. A more extreme type, the 'hi-lo' hub, enjoyed some support in the 1970s and Campagnolo hi-lo hubs of the era are highly sought after; the firm even offered a front hi-lo hub for use on the steep banking of a velodrome.

Function

The hub flange provides a location for the spokes. Historically, the most popular type has been the classic plate with holes drilled axially to accept J-bend spokes. This type has the advantage of being easy to machine on a lathe and allows the wheel builder freedom in choosing spoke lacing as the spokes can be angled for various crossings as they leave the flange.

Radial spoke lacing places great stress on the conventional hub flange, which can crack at the spoke holes and be torn away. Radial lacing should only be done with hubs either warranted to be able to withstand the additional stresses or designed specifically for the pattern. Keyhole drilling has been used as a solution to the problem of replacing a broken spoke in a conventional flange as it allows the spoke head to be passed through the flange from the spoke side. The shape of the hole weakens the flange and the design has fallen out of use in lightweight cycles.

▶ Holes in the disc-shaped hub flanges provide the classic location for J-bend spoke heads.

Construction

First tried on cycle wheels in the late 19th century, the stud flange is harder to manufacture than a plate but allows the use of straight-pull spokes, which avoid the potentially weakening bend at the head of a J-bend spoke. Instead, the mushroom head of the spoke pulls against the back of the stud or finger protruding from the hub barrel and, ideally, enjoys a straight path to the rim. The stud is usually drilled to accept the spoke but may be slotted so the spoke can be dropped into place without possible interference with others. As with keyhole drilling, this results in a weaker flange more susceptible to breakage. First generation Shimano wheels had their spoke nipples at the hub in stud flanges, requiring exceptional accuracy in machining to ensure that the spoke path from nipple to rim avoided any weakening kink and the need for such accuracy was one drawback of the stud flange.

Straight-pull radial spokes are often simply housed in a radial drilling or slot in the barrel, avoiding the need for a flange proper. This minimalist construction pares the front hub down to just three major constituent parts: the barrel, bearings and spindle. The rear must also have some means of carrying one or more drive sprockets.

Barrel

By far the most widely used technique for manufacturing the hub barrel is to machine it to shape from a single-piece forging or billet of aluminium alloy. Forging, which leaves the pre-machined 'blank' shaped roughly like the finished item, is used by major manufacturers as it creates a grain structure in the forged piece and is considered to create a stronger finished article. Aluminium alloy extruded in cylindrical billet form is less expensive and more readily available to smaller machine shops.

The hub can be made as a one-piece carbon-fibre moulding. The barrel and flanges can also be made separately and bonded together, offering the possibility of making them from different materials.

Aluminium remains favoured for the flanges as it is softer than stainless steel spokes and is well suited to housing bearing races. The barrel's purpose in a front hub is to keep the flanges apart and early Campagnolo hubs had a chromed steel barrel pressed into aluminium flanges. Titanium has been used to do the same job but carbon-fibre is more easily spotted and lighter and makes possible the use of a very large diameter barrel, usually in the rear hub. This adds valuable torsional rigidity and even allows the designer to put the rear wheel's tangent spokes on the non-drive side without risking the hub twisting under power.

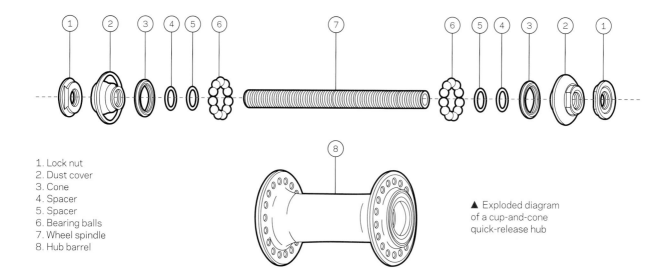

1. Lock nut
2. Dust cover
3. Cone
4. Spacer
5. Spacer
6. Bearing balls
7. Wheel spindle
8. Hub barrel

▲ Exploded diagram of a cup-and-cone quick-release hub

Bearings

By no means obsolete, cup-and-cone ball bearings are still used by Shimano in most road hubs. This type allows the bearings to be stripped for maintenance and adjustment of play if needed. They also resist axial loads more effectively than annular bearings, which are easily replaced when worn out but hard or impossible to service in pursuit of extended service life. Annular bearings are also inexpensive and readily available in a huge range of sizes and can be specified with seals or shields that keep out dirt and water. Both work equally well in cycle wheels, making choosing a hub on the basis of bearing type somewhat pointless.

Campagnolo's Record hub features cup-and-cone bearings and an oversized aluminium spindle inside a fat aluminium barrel. The bearings feature ceramic balls, which are lighter, harder and more spherical than steel and make Campagnolo's high-end hubs some of the smoothest-running in cycling today.

Spindle

Hidden away at the centre of the hub is the spindle, which on road bikes is usually hollow to accommodate the quick release skewer. Steel, the traditional choice on account of its strength, is increasingly being replaced by aluminium as an oversized aluminium spindle can be stiffer and lighter than steel. An aluminium spindle will usually run in annular bearings, which can be pressed in place without the need to cut a thread.

▶ Chris King's superb hubs are renowned for their smoothness and longevity.

Quick Release

At the summit of the Croce d'Aune is a monument to Italian Tullio Campagnolo, founder of the legendary cycle component company. It was on this challenging climb that he was moved to invent the wheel quick-release mechanism. Stuck in a snowstorm during the Gran Premio della Vittoria road race on 4th November 1924, Campagnolo could not undo his rear wheel with his frozen fingers and was unable to remove the rear wheel to change gear.

Wheel retention

The racing wheels of the era were secured using wingnuts, which in principle could be slackened using finger pressure alone. This practice saved carrying a spanner and having to produce it in a hurry when needed. Unfortunately, the need to ensure that the nuts would not come undone of their own accord meant that a rider might inadvertently apply an excessive tightening torque, leaving the nut hard to loosen by hand, even when warm.

Having decided something needed to be done, Campagnolo set about finding a solution and, in 1930, patented the quick-release wheel retention system still used today. It comprises a rod, or 'skewer', sliding inside a hollow wheel spindle. On one end is a thread and nut to permit fine adjustment of the system's bite point and of how hard it clamps. On the other is a lever-actuated eccentric cam that pulls the lever block up against the frame or fork dropouts. This then pulls the skewer through the spindle and the nut up against the opposing dropout, clamping the dropouts against the spindle-bearing locknuts. Small springs keep the nut and head equidistant from the faces of the dropouts to ensure rapid wheel fitment.

Skewer rod

Campagnolo's original design employed a small-diameter eccentric hidden inside the lever head, away from dirt and wear. To save on manufacturing costs, many quick-release skewers supplied with low-cost wheelsets site the eccentric on the outside of the lever, where it presses against a plastic or brass seat on the face of the head. This exposes the moving surfaces to dirt and grit and adds to friction. The tightening action is harder and less reassuring than that of an internal eccentric.

The skewer rod is made in either high-tensile steel or titanium. Steel skewers are heavier but, since titanium has a lower Young's modulus (see p. 16), also stiffer, since rods of both metals are of about the same diameter. This means that, in practice, a typical titanium skewer shaft will need to be stretched around 40% more to produce the same clamping force. The extra stretch must be supplied by the action of the eccentric and since lever length is usually unchanged, steel skewers give a much lighter closing action.

A cheaper and less effective way to tension the skewer is to use it as a very long, thin bolt with a fixed lever acting as a short spanner. Since the lever must be rotated through several turns to tighten the wheel, it is slower than a true quick release and requires space for the lever to move freely.

The temptation to overtighten the quick release should be resisted as it will stress the rod and apply undesirable axial load to the wheel bearings without adding to the security of the wheel. Clamping action should commence as the lever moves just past 90°; closing the lever does not require great force. Tradition says the quick release lever of both wheels should go on the left-hand side of the cycle. Most cyclists like to tuck it close to the fork blade or stays for neatness.

Freehub

Few riders who have ridden with them will remember the screw-on multiple freewheel, also known as a 'cluster' or 'block', with much fondness. It worked well enough in that it had several sprockets and a freewheel, but it was heavy and a pain to service. Which is why, of the many advances in component design ushered in by Shimano from the 1980s onwards, the freehub was arguably the most welcome.

◄ Splines on the freehub body transmit drive torque from the sprocket to the hub.

Freewheel mechanism

A Shimano trademark, 'Freehub' is also the generic term for a rear hub equipped with a splined sprocket carrier and integral freewheel. It was not the first hub to be fitted with an easily removable 'cassette' freewheel; the concept dates back to the 1930s. It was, however, the first to enjoy widespread acceptance and is now the industry standard.

Prior to its arrival, the multiple freewheel was the only option available to derailleur gear users. By the end of its reign, blocks with seven sprockets were available although the six-speed block was most popular. All such beasts screwed onto a threaded boss on the right-hand side of the rear hub. Removal required a heavy steel tool, equipped with either dogs or splines, that engaged with similar projections on the block and allowed the freewheeling portion to be held steady while the wheel was turned to unscrew the block.

Removal was but one problem caused by the arrangement. Its major drawback was the position in which it left the rear wheel hub bearings. Due to space considerations, these had to be placed inside the threaded boss and therefore closer than ideal to the wheel centre. To reach the right-hand rear dropout, the length of spindle outside the bearings was packed with spacers, creating a long tube placed under bending load somewhere close to its middle. No wonder even Campagnolo rear hub spindles were prone to bending.

With the introduction of the Freehub, Shimano banished all that nonsense. The device comprises a body attached coaxially to the hub barrel via a freewheel mechanism. Sealing the freewheel against dirt and water is, therefore, straightforward. In the Shimano implementation, the right-hand hub bearing sits close to the right-hand dropout to minimise bending loads on the spindle. Other freehub designs may not have this feature.

Freehub body

The body has splines on the outside over which slide the various rear sprockets and their associated spacers. The sprockets are secured in place by a lock ring threaded into the end of the body. On the early Shimano Dura-Ace design of 1978, the smallest, outside sprocket also served as the lockring. This was replaced by a more convenient splined lock ring in later versions. Sprocket removal is simple; while a chain whip is used to hold one of the sprockets and prevent the body from freewheeling backwards, a splined tool is used to remove the lockring, allowing the sprocket and spacers to be slid off.

Shimano's freehub bodies are, with the exception of a deep-splined aluminium Dura-Ace model that was quickly discontinued, made of either steel or titanium to resist indentation by the steel sprockets. Attempts to save weight by making the body in aluminium invariably fall foul of its relative softness. Chain tension torques the sprockets against the faces of the splines, creating localised pressure that may be enough to indent the body, hindering sprocket removal. Since weight at the hub is of marginal consequence to the performance of modern road bikes, steel may be considered the best material for the purpose unless the cost of titanium is acceptable.

FREEWHEEL VS FREEHUB

The freehub supports a collection of sprockets, or a 'cassette', on a freewheeling splined body forming an integral part of the hub. It superseded a system comprising a rear wheel hub with its barrel threaded to accept a screw-on multiple freewheel or 'block'.

1. Spindle
2. Lock nut
3. Dust cover
4. Bearing cone
5. Ball bearing
6. Bearing cup
7. Flanges with spoke holes
8. Spacer

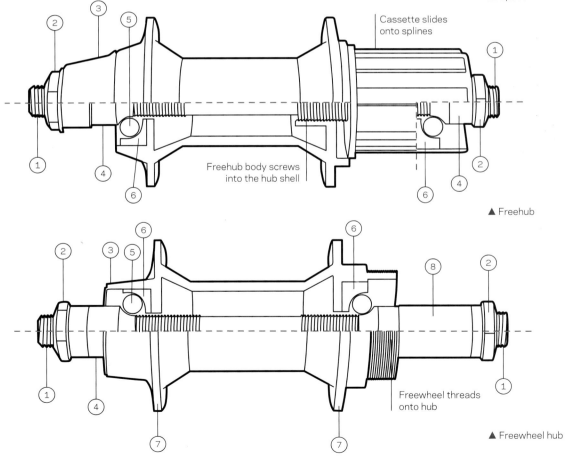

Cassette slides onto splines

Freehub body screws into the hub shell

▲ Freehub

Freewheel threads onto hub

▲ Freewheel hub

4

Drivetrain

The drivetrain is the train of components linking the power source and drive wheel or wheels. The best way to harness the meagre power output of even the most powerful of cyclists is a question that has inspired some of the most ingenious devices ever invented, many, such as the roller chain, useful in areas other than cycling. The same cannot be said of the derailleur gear change mechanism, which is associated with cycling and cycling alone.

Pedals: Shoe Cleats

Toppling over at a standstill having failed to unclip one's shoes from the pedals is something of a rite of passage for novice cyclists, as it takes time and practice for the sideways heel movement required to exit most 'clipless' road pedals to become an automatic action. Nevertheless, this rarely deters a new cyclist from plunging into the expensive world of dedicated cycling shoes and their pedals, for the improvement in performance they offer cannot be ignored.

Sole rigidity

Keen cyclists have always worn shoes specifically designed for the activity. They were doubtless first introduced because regular walking shoes are unsuitable; the bendy sole required for an easy, comfortable gait is too flexible to support the foot when pressing on narrow pedals, especially if of a lightweight steel-jaw racing pattern.

A stiff sole, then, is the first requirement of a proper cycling shoe. Touring shoes don't need an extremely rigid sole, since they are not expected to maximise performance and will certainly be used for some walking. Racing shoes, however, have always been made with as stiff as sole as practicable. Carved wooden soles were used by Italian manufacturers such as Duegi and Detto Pietro in the 1970s but the traditional stiffener was a thin strip of high-tensile or tool steel sandwiched between the layers of leather that made up the sole. At least one manufacturer was found to have used old saw blades for the purpose.

Cleat construction

To such a sole would be attached a 'cleat' with a slot that would fit over the back plate of a racing pedal. Once the toe strap was snugged tight, it became impossible to remove the shoe from the pedal without a hard upward tug, and with a deep cleat slot and tough straps, impossible even with one. The first action of a racing cyclist preparing to stop had to be a flick of the strap buckle to free its tension; the fall at traffic lights is not a new phenomenon.

Cleats, usually of cast light alloy for racing, were nailed to leather soles after a short ride in toe clips to let the pedal plate create an alignment mark. The cleat slot would usually be positioned about 3mm in front of the mark to ensure clearance between the toes and toe clips. Shoes fitted with metal cleats were useless for walking and therefore rarely had even a protective pad on the heel.

The use of hard plastic to make moulded soles meant that manufacturers could incorporate adjustable cleats. Such shoes, which became popular in the 1980s, were quickly adapted to take the new three-bolt clipless pedal cleats when they arrived in the mid-1980s. At the same time, the all-leather uppers of older racing shoes, which required endless care and maintenance, began to be replaced by synthetic mesh fabric with leather reinforcing bars. Shoes also began to be made with a moulded heel cup, which stiffened the heel as it was twisted to release the shoe from a clipless pedal.

By the end of the 1980s, laces had been largely replaced by Velcro® straps and the racing shoe of today was almost recognisable. With the introduction of super-stiff carbon-fibre soles fitted with supportive moulded footbeds and uppers secured with buckles and ratchet straps or, in some cases, nylon filament, the modern performance road cycling shoe was complete. Thanks to the presence on the sole of a large, rigid cleat, it remains as unsuited to walking as any of its ancestors, but that is surely an integral part of the appeal of dedicated cycling shoes.

CLEAT TYPES

Modern cleats for clipless pedal systems mostly fall into one of three types: two-bolt, which is mainly used for mountain bike shoes and pedals but increasingly seen in touring shoes suitable for walking; three-bolt, which originated with the LOOK clipless pedal and is most commonly found on 'road-type' cycling shoes; and four-bolt, which was introduced by TIME and is now almost obsolete as few shoes are made with suitable soles. It is still used by Speedplay but the firm's cleats usually require an adaptor to fit the three-bolt format.

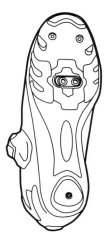

▲ Shoe for a 2-bolt pedal.

▲ Shoe for a 3-bolt pedal.

▲ Shoe for a 4-bolt pedal.

◄ Although designed for mountain biking, the recessed cleat of the twin-bolt system allows comfortable walking and is suitable for touring and commuting.

'Sportive' shoes and pedals

Tourists and leisure road riders can also take advantage of clipless convenience either by adopting mountain bike pedals and shoes or choosing from the new breed of road-orientated shoes and pedals constructed using the same technology. Both use a small cleat sitting in a recess between rubber blocks, keeping the cleat away from the ground. Most soles are sufficiently stiff to protect the foot from pedal pressure while allowing comfortable walking.

These 'sportive' shoes can be used with double-sided mountain bike pedals or, if appearance is important, with single-sided road pedals that use the same type of trap for the cleat. The performance of this combination falls not far short of that of low-cost road shoes and pedals, making it an attractive option for performance and leisure road cyclists alike.

Pedals: Clipless

In 1970 began a slow burning revolution that within 20 years had consigned to the bin a component that had been an integral part of performance cycling since the end of the 19th century. Cinelli's M71 pedal may have failed to capture much of the cycling market but it kicked off the concept of the modern 'clipless' pedal. The toe clip and its accompanying strap were on their way out.

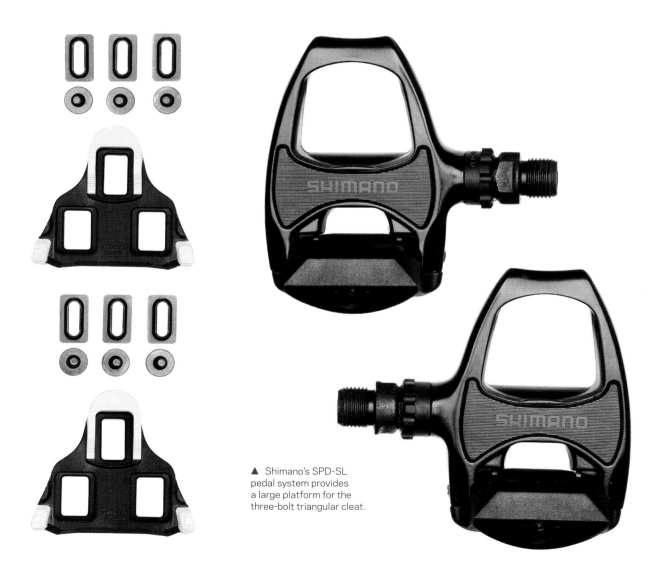

▲ Shimano's SPD-SL pedal system provides a large platform for the three-bolt triangular cleat.

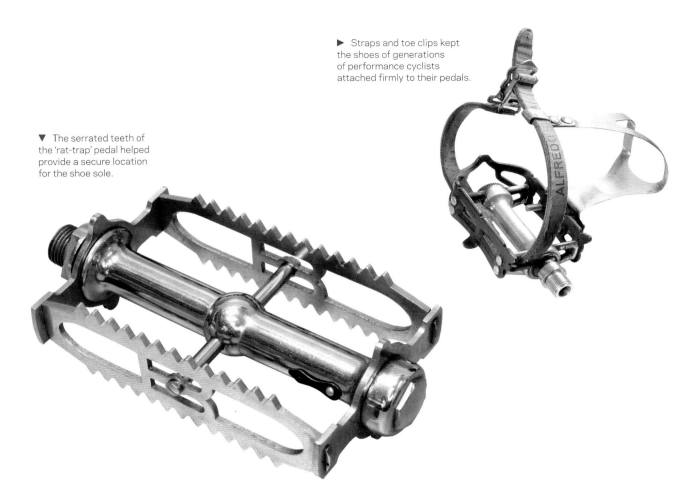

▲ The serrated teeth of the 'rat-trap' pedal helped provide a secure location for the shoe sole.

▶ Straps and toe clips kept the shoes of generations of performance cyclists attached firmly to their pedals.

Early pedal designs

Up until the arrival of the clipless road pedal in the 1970s, lightweight pedals were of three main types: the platform, the rat-trap and the quill.

Platform

The best known platform pedal was made in France by Lyotard and used from the 1930s onwards. Popular with touring cyclists, the design offered more support for the sole of the shoe than a quill or rat-trap and could still be used with toe clips and shallow cleats.

Rat-trap

Rat-trap pedals had sharp teeth to grip the shoe sole lining the edges of front and rear plates and could be used either way up, although the fitment of toe clips would preclude this. Rat-traps were almost always made of steel.

Quill

The quill pedal was a refinement of the rat-trap and featured an upturned nib on the outside intended to provide lateral location for the shoe. Since the pedal was designed to be used in one orientation, the front plate had holes for toe clip screws and the back had a small tongue used to flip

the pedal as the shoe was pushed inside the strap. The high point of quill pedal manufacture was reached with the Campagnolo Super Record design of the 1970s. Its titanium axle ran in precision cup-and-cone bearings protected from dirt and water by rifling on the axle. Hardened alloy was used for the quill plates, which had threaded holes for the toe clip screws. The later quill pedals often boasted aluminium alloy barrels. Quill pedals with one-piece cast aluminium bodies are still made today. Cup-and-cone bearings were used for the majority of these pedals but manufacturers such as TA offered needle roller or annular bearings from the early 1950s.

Typically, the pedals were fitted with Christophe toe clips and Binda straps. Early racing legend Eugene Christophe began manufacturing his clips in the 1920s and they remained the premier brand until clipless pedals took over. Multiple world champion and Giro d'Italia winner Alfredo Binda gave his name to straps preferred for their thick leather, sturdy buckle and long, stretch-free life. The clipless revolution put paid to all that.

Clipless function

The Cinelli M71 used a roughly square cleat with gently tapering, chamfered side edges, which slid forwards into a platform with raised, inward-leaning sides that gripped the cleat. To prevent the cleat pulling backwards, a manually operated tab pushed a button into the underside of the cleat. The reverse process released the cleat and shoe, making pedal exit a slow affair that needed plenty of forethought.

This was not the case with the clipless pedal that cracked the problem of entry and release. Based on a ski binding and invented by Jean Beyl, the LOOK PP65 pedal was introduced in 1984 and used by Bernard Hinault to win the 1985 Tour de France. This early proof of its capabilities ensured the pedal's rapid success amongst professional and amateur riders alike. By the early 1990s, only the great Sean Kelly among pro riders remained loyal to toe clips and an era was at an end.

Three-bolt cleat

LOOK's three-bolt cleat attachment format is now the standard pattern found on road shoe soles. The plastic cleat has a rounded nose and delta shape. At the rear, the edge is undercut to provide an engagement surface for the pedal's spring-loaded rear jaw. The profile of the cleat forces the jaw back against spring pressure both when treading down to engage and sideways to release from the pedal.

Early examples lacked the 'float' that allows the shoe to move around and change its orientation to the axle as the rider pedals. This was believed to contribute to the knee problems that afflicted some users and Beyl came up with a new design that offered a large degree of movement in the fore-and-aft and axial planes. When LOOK proved unwilling to proceed with the idea, Beyl parted company and set up the rival TIME concern to manufacture his TBT (TIME BioPerformance Technology) pedal, which was used by Tour de France winners Miguel Indurain and Greg LeMond.

The TBT design offered 7mm of lateral movement and a possible 5° of heel angle change either side of centred and was popular, but its multi-part cleat system required either a dedicated sole or an adaptor. Although TIME's TBT pedal has disappeared, its concept lives on in the firm's current iClic cleat retention system (see p. 89). The plastic cleat is in one piece, however, and fits the LOOK three-bolt sole format.

The TBT pedal lacked the simplicity of Beyl's earlier LOOK design, which was widely copied. Even today, LOOK's basic functionality remains unchanged although the current pedal range uses exotic materials to save weight. The design was manufactured under licence by Shimano and Campagnolo and forms the basis of low-cost road pedals by manufacturers such as Wellgo.

LOOK's design may be the most widely used of road pedal systems, but it is not perfect even now. Float is centred on the toe of the cleat, leading to a wide range of heel movement for a small change of foot position. The cleat adds to 'stack' height, or the distance of the foot above the pedal axle centre, and becomes mis-shapen with wear, altering foot angle with the pedal.

Of the many attempts to build a better road pedal, the most convincing is surely the Speedplay concept, which was patented in 1989 by Richard Byrne. Popular with professional racers and enthusiast road cyclists, it comprises a circular, double-sided pedal platform that sits in a recess in the cleat, which is screwed to the shoe sole. This places the sole as close to the pedal as possible; needle roller bearings reduce the thickness of the pedal body while maintaining load-carrying ability. The circular shape of the pedal allows free rotation about the centre of the pedal, minimising heel movement. The current Zero version of the pedal offers the choice of limited float and even fixed cleat positioning.

As ever, there's a trade-off; the pedal is small and light, but the cleat, which contains the trap mechanism, is large and difficult to walk in.

◀ Careful attention to detail has given road pedals a remarkably sleek profile.

CLIPLESS PEDAL TYPES

The most widely used 'clipless' road pedals are those made by LOOK, TIME and Speedplay. They are designed to offer a secure housing for the shoe cleat, to provide a large supporting surface to transmit pedal force and to permit ready release of the cleat. Shimano's popular PD-A520 pedal combines the looks of a single-sided road pedal with the convenience of a mountain bike-style shoe sole.

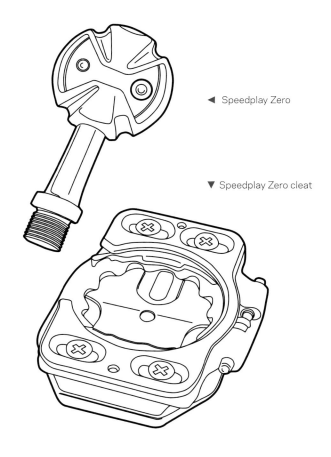

◀ Speedplay Zero

▼ Speedplay Zero cleat

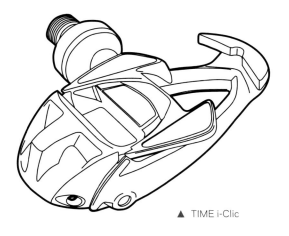

▲ TIME i-Clic

▼ Shimano PD-A520

▼ LOOK Keo

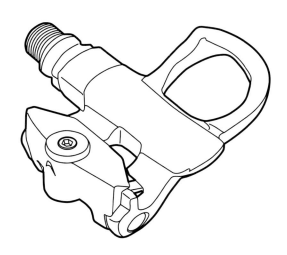

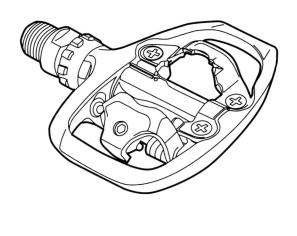

Chainset

Strictly speaking, the chainset includes the bottom bracket axle and bearings but here we look at the chainrings, the crank arms and their interface with the axle. The chainset is the powerhouse of the road bike, responsible for harnessing the rider's energy and delivering it to the drivetrain. Its effectiveness depends on structural and mechanical efficiency and on its relationship with the rider's physiological particulars.

Cotter pin crank

Until the 1950s, the crank arms, or cranks, were made of steel and connected to the axle by means of a device known as the cotter pin.

Thankfully obsolete but likely to be familiar to owners of vintage lightweight road bikes, the cotter pin is a short length of round mild steel rod with a flat on one side and an offset male threaded screw. The flat on the pin bears against a flat on the axle and is angled to form a wedge so that, as the pin is driven through the hole on the head of the crank, it jams the crank and axle together. A nut and washer on the screw keep the pin in place.

While generally reliable if well set-up, the system presents a number of potential problems. The flats on the pins must be filed prior to fitment and at an identical angle or the cranks will not sit at precisely 180°. Removing the pins without damaging them is difficult as it may require a hammer, and there's the vexed question of direction of

rotation. Both nut-forward and head-forward rotation once had their advocates although it is clear that, since one of the two functions of the pins is to transmit torque from the left-hand crank via the axle, it cannot matter at this point as the pins experience opposite loadings.

Ugly though cotter pins are, they do not necessarily prevent a cottered steel chainset from looking very pleasing. Slender of profile and given a shiny plating of chrome, solid steel cranks may rival aluminium cranks by Campagnolo for visual appeal. Most high-end steel cranks, even when intended for competition, were solid, but beautiful hollow steel cranks were made by firms such as Duprat. While light, such cranks tend to be somewhat flexible and better suited to touring than racing.

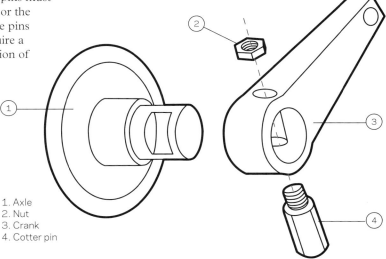

1. Axle
2. Nut
3. Crank
4. Cotter pin

CRANK LENGTH

Crank length has been the subject of debate since cyclists were freed by the invention of the safety bicycle to ride cranks as long as they liked. By the early 1900s, adventurous cyclists were trying ever longer cranks; one theory prevalent in the UK at the time contended that crank length should be one tenth of the gear size in inches (see p. 123).

With the advent of variable gearing, arguments about crank length died down and manufacturers generally settled on lengths of between 165mm and 170mm. Cranks as long as 177.5mm were used by racing cyclists hoping to find a competitive advantage; longer cranks were usually favoured for time trialling.

Crank arms today are manufactured in a range of lengths to suit riders with various leg lengths and pedalling styles. Common lengths include 165mm, 170mm, 172.5mm and 175mm. 177.5mm and 180mm cranks can also be found without too much difficulty. 172.5mm is the length most widely fitted to new road bikes and suits the majority of riders.

Cotterless crank

The stresses created by the wedging action of the cotter pin make it unsuitable for use with aluminium cranks. In contrast, the square-taper 'cotterless' system was found to be better suited to aluminium than steel. Any crank that is not connected using a cotter pin may be described as cotterless, of course, although the term is now outdated. One of the best early designs, by Williams, employed an axle with tapered splines. A square taper, however, proved easier to machine on the end of the axle and was the pattern universally adopted for light alloy cotterless cranks.

The square taper hole in steel cotterless cranks such as those made by a number of firms including Cinelli and Gnutti proved prone to wear, perhaps because any mismatch between equally hard mating surfaces would result in a poor fit. A relatively soft aluminium crank is able to conform to a snug fit over a steel – or titanium – axle, resulting in a secure and reliable connection.

Provided, that is, the crank is correctly installed. Square-taper is a simple technology but requires a sturdy crank head to resist the wedge action of the taper. The wedge effect also affects installation. If fitted 'dry', without lubrication, the faces of crank and axle may gall or cold-weld, preventing the crank from pressing fully home on the taper. Better is to oil the faces of the axle before installation so the crank can slide home freely. Provided the bolt is not over-tightened, elastic deformation of the alloy will allow the crank to grip the axle and press against the bolt head, preventing it coming loose.

Square-taper aluminium cranks have served road cycling well for over 50 years and remain an excellent choice for all but the most competitive of cycling activities. Keep the crank bolts snug but not over-tight, oil the axle tapers and use the extractor tool for removal and a square-taper crankset will give years of service.

If using one, it is worth noting that there are two main square-taper standards: JIS, used by Japanese manufacturers and US brands and ISO, used by Europeans. The taper is the same at 2° to the axle centre line but the JIS taper is longer, as is the hole in the crank head. Ideally, they should not be mixed but an ISO crank will go on a JIS axle without too much problem.

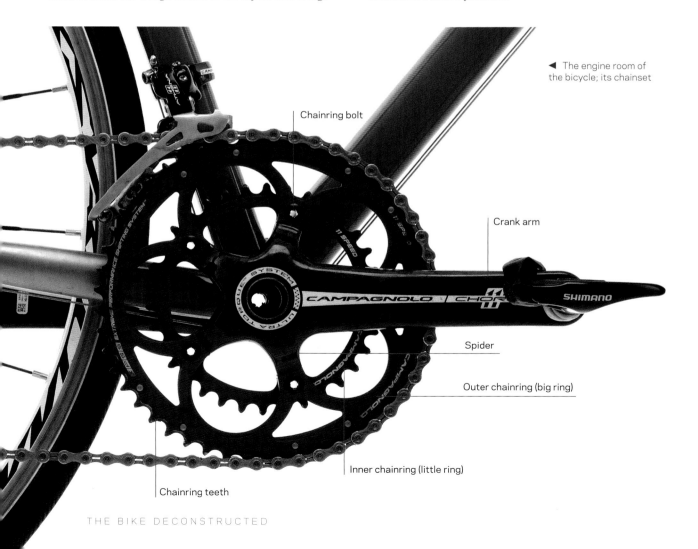

◀ The engine room of the bicycle; its chainset

Chainring bolt

Crank arm

Spider

Outer chainring (big ring)

Inner chainring (little ring)

Chainring teeth

Crank axle

Progress in crank-axle interface design is aimed at losing weight without compromising on stiffness. The Williams splined design proved ahead of its time as, in the 1990s, manufacturers widely adopted a splined attachment system. Splines transfer torque without generating the excessive radial stresses of the square taper and therefore require less material to be used in the crank head.

Shimano's eight-spline Octalink crankset and the 10-spline 'open standard' ISIS Drive design it inspired had steel axles of larger diameter than seen with square-taper but located on bearings placed inside the bracket shell.

These designs were made obsolete by the arrival of Shimano's Hollowtech II system. Its oversized axle is a fixed part of the right-hand crank assembly, saving weight and adding rigidity by obviating the requirement for a separable, potentially flexible interface. The left-hand crank fits over fine splines on a parallel-sided axle. It is pulled against the face of the outboard bearing by a cap and secured by bolts that pinch the crank around the axle.

It inspired imitators using the same fixed axle and outboard bearing layout. Campagnolo's Ultra-Torque system avoids looking too similar by using a half-axle fixed in each crank but the newer Power-Torque design follows established practice with its axle fixed to the right-hand crank.

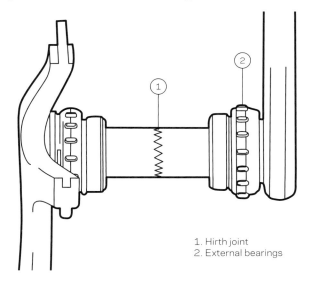

1. Hirth joint
2. External bearings

▲ Campagnolo Ultra-Torque bottom bracket axle and bearings

Crank arm construction

A firm connection with the axle deserves a rigid crank arm. The way most riders pedal on the down stroke applies force to the crank from various directions as the pedal travels around its circle. Even the smoothest of cyclists to some extent applies radial force to the pedal, and the combination of this with the useful tangential pedalling force twists and bends the crank along the axis between pedal and bottom bracket axles.

Hollow arm

As the pedal and bottom bracket axles are on opposite sides, the crank arm needs to be stiff in torsion as well as in bending. The traditional solid aluminium arm is stiffer than a solid steel crank but a hollow arm is better. A hollow arm of substantial cross section is even better than a regular one that has simply had a hole bored through it, and the latest generation aluminium cranks are massive.

While hollow crank arms are not new, it was the Cannondale-owned CODA's machined and bonded cranks that really pushed their design and manufacture in aluminium. The cranks were attached to a machined aluminium axle via eight lobular, or rounded, splines; the construction technique was so advanced it is still used by Cannondale today for the System Integrated (SI) Hollowgram crankset. This is claimed by Cannondale to be the best performing crankset on the market but can only be fitted to frames built for the BB30 bottom bracket format.

Shimano's first hollow road crank offering was derived from the eight-speed XTR mtb groupset. The Dura-Ace 7700 cranks were made by forging a U-channel and welding aluminium sheet to the back of it. The technique produces a light finished item but it is difficult to ensure the consistency of the weld. The model was followed by Ultegra and even 105 designs that were heavier but much less expensive to manufacture, although the techniques used to do so were kept secret.

Unveiled in 2003, the Dura-Ace 7800 crankset not only represented an even greater leap in performance but entirely rethought the aesthetics of road bike components. Carried on by Shimano across numerous groupsets through to the current Dura-Ace 9000 group, the design of the right-hand crank dumps the traditional visual reference of a centre bolt and replaces it with an uninterrupted surface from pedal to chainring spider. It is bold and unmistakeable.

So light and rigid are hollow aluminium crank arms that other manufacturers have looked for ways to make them. The arms of Rotor's 3D series of cranksets are lightened by means of a manufacturing process known as Trinity Drilling System. Three holes are drilled along the length of an extruded aluminium alloy bar to leave a triple chamber cross-section arm of immense stiffness. It is a major improvement on the Hollowminum technology used in the Spanish firm's earlier Agilis crankset. With slender arms and one central hole, the Agilis design is, like Duprat's hollow steel cranks, elegant but comparatively flexible.

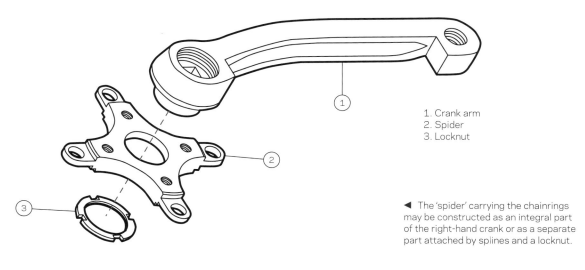

1. Crank arm
2. Spider
3. Locknut

◀ The 'spider' carrying the chainrings may be constructed as an integral part of the right-hand crank or as a separate part attached by splines and a locknut.

Material

Attempts to make reliable crank arms in carbon-fibre took a long time to come to fruition. The difficulty of connecting the ends of the crank to the pedal and bottom bracket axles for a long time presented a major stumbling block. The potential of the material for making light and stiff cranks encouraged major manufacturers with the notable exception of Shimano to persevere and reliable, elegant carbon-fibre cranks now lead the product ranges of manufacturers from Campagnolo and SRAM to FSA. Their performance is comparable to that of the best aluminium cranks.

For an idea of the possibilities available with carbon-fibre chainset construction, look no further than French manufacturer LOOK's unique ZED2. The cranks and axle are moulded in one piece with a large-diameter centre section rotating in 64mm ID bearings, which permit the assembly to be passed through the bracket shell during installation. Although exceptionally stiff and light, the ZED2 crankset is only compatible with LOOK's 695 frameset.

Chainrings

The single chainring on early road bikes was invariably stamped from sheet or cut from cast steel. Steel remained the preferred material for high-end cycles until the 1930s, when aluminium chainrings began to find favour. Aluminium has the obvious advantage of being light in weight but also scores on stiffness, as an aluminium ring can be cut out of thicker plate. Steel rings were often provided with a stiffening flange to prevent flex and even buckling. Axial stiffness is especially important when using derailleur gears, which apply a sideways pull to the chain in all but one or two sprockets.

It was soon found that, although even the hardest aluminium alloys are softer than steel, aluminium rings wear more slowly. This is thought to be either because the softer metal quickly assumes the precise shape of the chainring teeth to make a better fit or because hard silica dust and grit particles become embedded in the soft alloy, creating a super-hard wear-resistant surface.

Despite their merits, aluminium chainrings were only slowly adopted for performance cycling and even during the 1950s steel rings remained popular within professional racing. The next question facing crankset manufacturers concerned the best way to attach the chainring or rings to the right-hand crank. Many manufacturers in the 1930s opted for the practice of fitting the right-hand crank with a small-diameter flanged boss. The chainring fitted over the boss and was fixed to the flange using five bolts.

Used through to the 1980s by French components specialists TA and Stronglight, this pattern allows the fitment of small chainrings suitable for touring. TA's Cyclotouriste chainrings fitted the crank pattern and could be set up as a triple chainset; the same firm's Criterium chainrings also fitted and were supposedly made for racing, although the cranks lacked the rigidity of proper competition components.

Bolt circle diameter (BCD)

By the 1950s, Italian manufacturers generally preferred to attach chainrings to a 'spider' with long arms and a large BCD.

This arrangement had the effect of limiting inner chainring minimum size and was, therefore, best suited to racing, where low gears were not thought necessary. In exchange, the substantial arms of the spider added rigidity.

Chainrings are fixed to the crank spider using a number of chainring bolts, usually five. These usually lie on a circle of a diameter known as the BCD or bolt circle diameter. The 53/39 'standard' chainring pairing usually fitted to competition road bikes requires a 130mm BCD (Campagnolo uses 135mm) while sportive and touring bikes may use a 'compact' 110mm BCD fitted with a 50/34 tooth chainring combination.

The trend of the late 1990s towards fitting triple chainrings stalled with the industry's adoption of the 'compact' chainset. Triple chainsets, with three chainrings, are popular for touring because they offer some very low gear ratios in addition to the standard road range. They have lost ground recently with the introduction of 10-speed rear cassettes, which provide a similarly wide range of ratios. SRAM's extra-low ratio WiFLi transmission, which has a 34 x 32 lowest gear ratio, is specifically designed to appeal to potential triple chainset users.

The BCD of Campagnolo's models got smaller over time; the 1958 Record chainset had a 151mm BCD and 44-tooth minimum inner chainring size; this was reduced to 144mm and 41 teeth respectively 10 years later.

Today's road bike-specific chainsets are generally designed for racing or sportive use and do not permit the fitment of chainrings smaller than 33 teeth.

CHAINRING SHAPES

Oval and other non-circular chainrings have been fitted to chain-driven bicycles since the early days of the safety bicycle. An oval chainring named the Thetic was well received during the 1930s and there has been a recent revival in the idea led by Rotor and O symmetric. The general principle is to orientate the long axis of the ring to pull on the chain at the point in the pedal stroke when the rider applies most force. Conversely, the crank swings quickly through the 'dead spot' in the pedal's rotation.

Non-circular chainring shapes can be very complex as designers try to harness the rider's power most efficiently. Used by 2012 Tour de France winner Sir Bradley Wiggins, who rode on O symmetric rings, their reputation has never been higher although their effectiveness remains subject to debate.

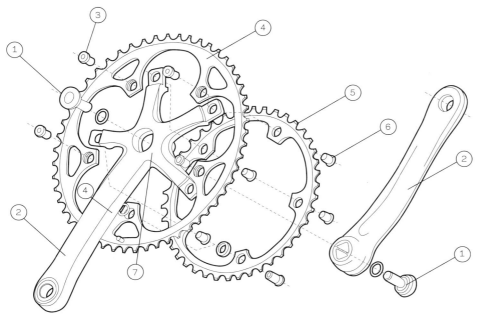

◀ The crank arms and chainrings are connected using several, usually five, small chainring bolts.

1. Crank bolt
2. Crank arm
3. Chainring bolt
4. Outer chainring
5. Inner chainring
6. Outer chainring bolt
7. Spider

Bottom Bracket Assemblies

Expected to be able to transmit the enormous pedalling forces applied by hulking sprinters, the bottom bracket axle is the hardest working component in a road bike. Failures are rare but, when they happen, the results are invariably painful and potentially fatal; it must be reliable. The bottom bracket assembly comprises the axle including its interface with the crank arms, the bearings and the bearing housings.

Bottom bracket shell

Traditionally, cups threaded into the bottom bracket shell were used as both bearing race and housing. With this arrangement, the shell plays a large part in determining the size and type of bearings that can be used and, consequently, the axle design itself. In particular, the diameter of the standard bottom bracket shell is seen by many engineers as one of the major limiting factors in cycle design.

It was arrived at early in the evolution of the safety bicycle and chosen as the size that would accommodate in acceptably durable ball bearings a solid steel axle sufficiently rigid for racing. The two most common shell sizes are British, which has an internal diameter of just under 35mm and takes cups with a 1.37in x 24tpi thread and Italian, which takes cups with a 36 x 24tpi thread.

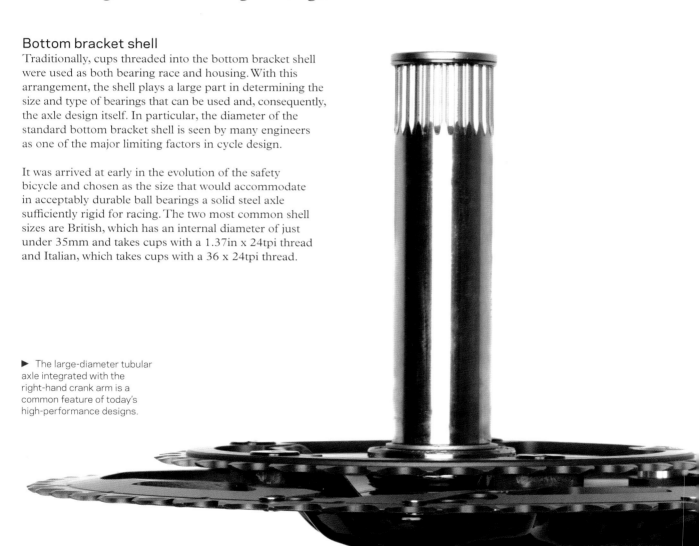

▶ The large-diameter tubular axle integrated with the right-hand crank arm is a common feature of today's high-performance designs.

Axle rotation

Threaded bearing cups are marked with the thread size and, in the case of British threaded cups, with its direction, since the right-hand cup has a left-hand thread. This is to prevent it unscrewing in use due to the effect of annular precession; as the axle rotates, the point at which pedal pressure is applied to the cup travels around it, generating a tendency for the cup to rotate in the opposite direction to the axle. It can be imagined by rotating a pencil around the inside of the looped index finger and thumb; the pencil will rotate backwards as it travels forwards around the loop.

As the right-hand cup in an Italian-format bottom bracket shell has a right-hand thread and will tend to come loose, it must be tightened with great force. Recognising the problem, some Italian cycle manufacturers use the British format; the venerable firm of Bianchi has always done so.

The right-hand cup of an old British-threaded assembly has a flange that bears against the side of the shell when the cup is tightened. This makes it 'fixed' as it cannot be turned to adjust bearing play. Instead, this is done using the left-hand cup, which is secured with a lock ring once axle bearing play is correctly adjusted.

One annoying feature of the bearing type is the difficulty of discerning free play by holding the axle. A useful trick is to attach the right-hand crank the axle and feel for play through the end of the crank, which, being further from the bearing surfaces, exhibits a greater degree of movement for the same amount of bearing play.

A Sturmey-Archer hub sprocket shim can be placed behind the flange of the right-hand cup to move it away from the shell should it be felt necessary to alter the spacing of the pedal 'tread'. On some cranksets, the right-hand crank may be found to be closer to the seat tube than the left-hander; using a shim shifts both cranks sideways to the right by the width of the shim. The balancing effect is, therefore, double the thickness of the shim.

Old-style cup-and-cone or 'loose' ball bearing bottom bracket assemblies employ 11 balls per side. The 22 quarter-inch balls run loose, or uncaged, in their cups; assembly usually requires the use of grease to hold the balls in place while the axle is installed. The grease, of course, is needed for lubrication but when the system was used for competition some mechanics would run the balls in oil in an attempt to save the small amount of power lost to pushing them through grease. In this case, assembly could prove taxing.

▶ Campagnolo Ultra-Torque bottom bracket cups

1. Outboard bearing
2. Retaining clip
3. Outboard bearing
4. Wave washer
5. Cup seal

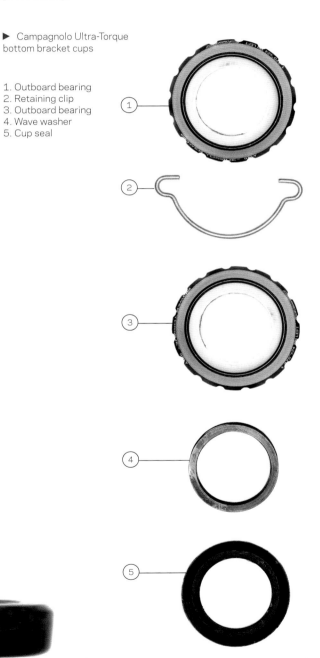

Axle

An axle designed for loose bearings has a pair of flanges that form the inner, or cone, bearing faces. The ends of the axle are provided with some means of attachment to the cranks such as cotter pins or a square taper (see pp. 91–93).

Until very recently the axle itself was always made in high-tensile steel. It needs to be both strong and stiff as it must transmit the pedalling force applied to the left-hand crank to the right-hand crank spider and thence to the chainring. For efficient power transfer the axle must be torsionally stiff so that it does not twist noticeably along its length (see p. 101).

The limitation on axle diameter imposed by standard bearing cup size makes steel the best material for use in a traditional assembly. Early attempts to take advantage of titanium's light weight were abandoned following French cyclist Laurent Fignon's fall in 1982 near the end of the Blois–Chaville classic road race. His titanium Campagnolo Super Record axle snapped, leaving him winded in the middle of the road when he had been in a potentially race-winning solo break. Today, reliable titanium axles designed for use inside a standard shell are made by a few small companies such as Royce in the UK and the metal now has a good reputation used as a bottom bracket axle.

Just prior to the almost industry-wide adoption of external bottom bracket bearings, Campagnolo attempted to surmount the traditional limitations on axle diameter by making for the mid-1990s Record crankset a steel axle with an oversized central bulge. The axle had to be hollow, of course, and was machined in two halves which were then friction-welded together. Although an improvement on the previous axle once manufacturing difficulties had been overcome, it was quickly rendered obsolete.

Of the numerous attempts to improve on the simple cup-and-cone bottom bracket assembly, few gained much public acceptance until the development of the Shimano all-in-one cartridge type, which arguably succeeded thanks to mountain biking as it offered fairly effective sealing against the ingress of water and dirt. Earlier 'sealed' bearing units such as the Bayliss Wiley design of the late 1940s and the aluminium-shell Nadax of the 1980s demonstrated no clear advantage over the loose-bearing system, which is easy to dismantle for maintenance and adjustable in the case of minor wear.

The pinnacle of cup-and-cone assembly development was reached with the Campagnolo Nuovo Record design. First appearing in 1967, it featured the legendary Italian firm's usual tight-tolerance balls and superlative finish and cups with rifled openings for the axle, which directed water outwards and away from the bearings as the axle rotated. A concertina plastic sleeve fitted between the cups kept water running down the inside of the seat tube from reaching the bearings.

▶ Race Face ISIS drive cartridge bottom bracket assembly

▼ Cartridge bottom bracket assembly with square-taper axle

▼ Shimano Octalink cartridge bottom bracket assembly

◀ Shimano all-in-one bottom bracket assembly

Outboard bearings

Keeping the bottom bracket bearings tucked away inside the standard sized bracket shell severely limits axle diameter, which in turn means that the axle needs very thick walls in order to provide adequate torsional stiffness.

Shimano first attempted to get around the problem with the Dura-Ace 7700 assembly, which uses a larger-diameter 'Octalink' axle turning in a combination of ball and roller bearing elements inside aluminium cups. Required simply to provide axial location, the balls are tiny while the assembly itself is complex and expensive to manufacture.

It proved a complex and expensive approach unsuitable for the firm's lower-cost groupsets of the day, which employed a similarly fat axle running in undersized cartridge bearings with reduced load carrying ability and therefore durability. The similar ISIS Drive bottom bracket also uses an all-in-one cartridge with smaller, less durable bearings.

In 2003, Shimano unveiled the 7800 Dura-Ace groupset. Its Hollowtech II crankset ran in bearings placed outside the bottom bracket shell in a manner pioneered in the early 1990s by Magic Motorcycle and later marketed by Cannondale under the CODA label. Bearings located outside the shell do not limit axle diameter. Hollowtech II and other outboard bearings of similar design such as Truvativ's GXP use a 24mm diameter axle. As the torsional stiffness of a tube increases as the fourth power of its radius, an oversized axle with thinner tube walls can be made stiffer and lighter than standard depending on material.

Hollowtech II bearings sit in aluminium housings with threaded sleeves as do those of Truvativ's GXP, Rotor's BSA and other variants on the theme. The housings fit standard British or Italian threaded shells, depending on thread, making them compatible with most road bikes.

Campagnolo's Ultra-Torque bottom bracket cups are screwed into the shell but the bearings themselves are pressed directly onto half-axles integral with the cranks. Ringing the changes, the firm's later Power-Torque design adopts the single-piece axle integral with the right-hand crank favoured by other manufacturers. While the right-hand bearing is pressed onto the axle, the left-hand bearing sits pre-fitted in the left-hand cup.

Ceramic bearings are increasingly used for the bottom bracket assembly. Campagnolo and SRAM both offer them as standard while a number of aftermarket manufacturers offer them as a replacement for the manufacturer's offering. The balls are formed of silicon nitride (Si_3N_4) and are not only about 30% lighter than steel equivalents but more spherical for smoother running and harder so they lose less energy to elastic deformation. They are widely claimed to be longer lasting but some authorities dispute this, pointing out that ceramic bearings are designed for high-speed, low-torque applications, which are exactly the opposite of the conditions experienced by cycle bottom bracket bearings.

The outboard bottom bracket assembly for a 24mm axle is now the most commonly used industry standard. It is widely compatible, is easily replaced in the event of failure and has ensured that cycles fitted with a conventional threaded bottom bracket shell remain competitive against machines with more recent bracket layouts.

AXLE TWIST

Although the terms 'axle' and 'spindle' are widely used interchangeably, it makes some sense to allocate to each a distinct meaning Throughout this book 'axle' means a shaft that rotates relative to the cycle frame, e.g. bottom bracket axle, and 'spindle' one that does not, e.g. wheel spindle.

The bottom bracket axle is stressed in torsion when turning force is applied to the left-hand pedal. At a rough calculation, a 20kg (44lb) tangent pedal force applied to the left-hand crank instantaneously twists a conventional steel axle by a little more than one quarter of one degree. A 24mm diameter steel axle for outboard bearings is about 16% stiffer and roughly the same weight. Cannondale's Hollowgram 2 BB30 aluminium axle is some 40% stiffer and 30% lighter.

Press-fitted

There are a number of bottom bracket standards competing today with the threaded outboard type for the cycle manufacturer's favour. They are based on the idea of using annular cartridge bearings press-fitted directly into the bottom bracket shell, which must be manufactured to suit.

They include Cannondale's BB30 and its BB30 Pressfit sibling, BB386Evo and Cervélo's BBRight. They differ in detail and in the bottom bracket shell type required.

BB30

Cannondale developed BB30 from the CODA design. It uses the same 6806 cartridge bearings to house a 30mm diameter axle that interfaces with BB30-specific cranks via an eight-lobe taper. BB30 is an open standard that can be used by any manufacturer. Some BB30 cranksets e.g. FSA have the axle permanently embedded in the right-hand crank. The BB30 axle is usually machined from aluminium; steel has been used to add weight if a pro race bike needs to be ballasted to meet the UCI minimum weight limit. The system requires a frame with BB30 bottom bracket shell, which is 68mm wide and bored to 41.96mm ID to accept the cartridge bearings as a press fit.

BB30 Pressfit

Otherwise identical to BB30, it requires less precise bottom bracket shell manufacture, using plastic inserts pressed into a 46mm ID bracket shell to house the 42mm OD bearings. The soft plastic inserts can conform to imperfections left by inaccurate machining of an aluminium bracket shell. Pressfit BB30 is also preferred over regular BB30 for use in carbon-fibre frames as the larger surface area of the inserts improves the fit between the bearings and frame.

BBRight

Initiated by Cervélo, BBRight is supposed to improve on BB30. It has a 30mm OD axle and uses 6806 bearings but requires a wider bracket shell and, requiring a dedicated BBRight crankset, is rarely seen on anything but Cervélo's own machines. The bracket shell is wider by 11mm on the non-drive side so that the bearing sits directly against the crank. The right-hand bearing is in the same position relative to frame centre line as with BB30, 11mm closer to the frame centre line. Shell width is therefore 79mm and the right-hand crank has to be spaced outwards by 11mm to ensure correct chainline.

▼ BB30 Pressfit bearings sit in plastic sleeves which are pressed into the non-threaded bottom bracket shell.

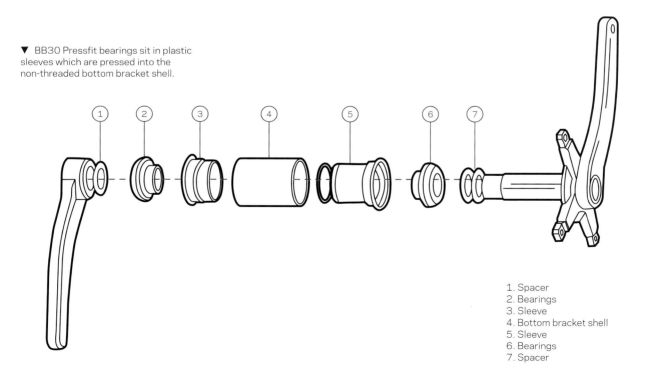

1. Spacer
2. Bearings
3. Sleeve
4. Bottom bracket shell
5. Sleeve
6. Bearings
7. Spacer

BB86

First introduced by Scott in collaboration with Shimano, and since used by other manufacturers, it employs 6805 outboard-type bearings pressed into the frame and works with Hollowtech II-type cranksets. Shimano's SM-BB91 Road Press Fit Bottom Bracket fits frames with a bottom bracket shell width of 86.5mm, hence the BB86 code, the flanges adding the required width. The BB86 bearings are retained in a hard plastic shell that is pressed into sockets net-moulded in the frame.

BB90

BB90 is Trek's 'proprietary' standard and uses 6806 bearings – the same as those in Hollowtech II outboard housings – pressed directly into net-moulded sockets in the carbon-fibre moulding around the bracket and is compatible with any Hollowtech II-type crankset. The advantage over a threaded shell is that the bearings sit directly in the frame instead of in a metal housing. This also removes the need to put a threaded metal insert in a carbon-fibre frame.

▼ Campagnolo Chorus outboard bearings on a traditional 68mm bottom bracket shell.

Chains

The roller chain's exceptional efficiency, rated at 98.4% by the National Physical Laboratory, makes it the most effective means of transmitting power devised for cycling. Carbon-fibre-reinforced belt drives offer a viable but expensive, low-maintenance alternative but absorb a little more power and are unsuitable for use with derailleur gears, leaving the roller chain the preferred choice for both utility and performance road cycling.

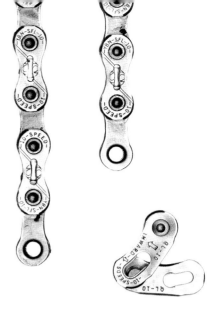

▲ A 'master' link comprising opposite-sided plates with pins slotting in keyholes is often used to join derailleur chains.

History

The bush roller chain was invented by Swiss engineer Hans Reynold in 1880 and by 1890 had, thanks to its smoother running and greatly improved performance, largely replaced the block chains first fitted to tricycles and safety bicycles.

Chain size depends on pitch, which is the distance between successive pins, and width, which is the distance between the inside faces of the inner side plates. The ½in pitch and ⅛in width format was the size quickly adopted for cycle use although it was briefly challenged in 1910 by the 8mm pitch Coventry Chain Co.'s Chainette and in 1979 by Shimano's 10mm pitch transmission.

The ⅛in roller chain used for utility, fixed-wheel and track racing cycles lacks the lateral flexibility needed for derailleur gearing. The narrower and more flexible ³⁄₃₂in chain needed for derailleurs with five or more sprockets first appeared in France towards the end of the 1930s and was only superseded in 1978 when Sedis launched the legendary Sedisport 4D chain.

Derailleur chains

Considerably lighter and offering greatly improved flexibility, shifting, strength and durability, the Sedisport instantly rendered all opposition obsolete. Virtually all derailleur chain sold today is of the same 'bushless' pattern. The standard roller chain has inner side plates pressed firmly over bushes with the rollers on the outside and the pins of the outer plates on the inside. This creates a smooth running but laterally rigid assembly. If flexed sideways, it puts all load on the sharp edges of the bushes, which bear against the pins, creating rapid wear and risk of breakage.

The Sedisport chain discarded the inner plate bushings in favour of inner plates each stamped with two short tubular protrusions on their inner faces. The outer plate pins pass through the protrusions while the rollers bear against them. The profiles of the roller inner surfaces and side plate protrusions spread the load and ensure excellent lateral flexibility.

As manufacturers have added more rear sprockets, derailleur chain has become progressively narrower across the outside thanks to improvements in material strength while retaining the same internal width. Chain should be used with the appropriate sprocket count to avoid risk of the side plates fouling adjacent sprockets.

The split link with the spring clip used to connect a one-eighth chain is too wide for use with a derailleur system and the ³⁄₃₂in chain used with early derailleurs had to be broken and joined by pressing any pin through the outer plate, relying on friction to keep the pin in place.

Most derailleur chains are supplied today with a quick fastening 'master' link comprising two asymmetric halves that connect to form an outer link. The ends of the pins pass through and interlock with keyholes in the opposing side plates to form a secure connection.

ROLLER CHAIN

The roller chain improves on the efficiency of other types thanks to the reduction in friction afforded as the roller engages with and leaves the sprocket tooth, rolling into position instead of sliding. Efficiency is affected by lack of lubrication and contamination by dirt and wear. Sprocket teeth can wear into a hooked shape with a ramped wear face that forces the chain to climb the ramp as it transmits power, wasting energy. Wear to the chain itself takes place between the pins and bushes or, in the case of modern derailleur chains, between the pins and side plates, leading to an increase in chain pitch that can be measured along a length of chain as 'stretch'.

As a rule, a chain should be replaced when it stretches by 1% to prevent early wear to the sprockets. This can be checked easily by measuring across 24 pins; unworn, they will cover 12in; worn by 1%, 12⅛in. There are several chain checking devices available that make an accurate assessment of chain wear.

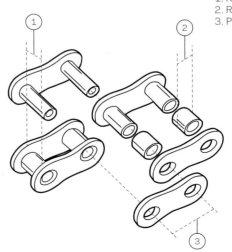

1. Roller diameter
2. Roller width
3. Pitch

Derailleur Gears

Somebody once said of the derailleur gear: 'C'est brutal, mais ça marche'. It is true; the concept of changing gear ratios by derailing the chain from one chainwheel to another of a different size is indeed brutal. But it does work and, importantly from the cyclist's viewpoint, it consumes little more energy than a single-speed transmission.

Form and function

The basic requirements of a derailleur gear system are few: it needs a multiple freewheel, a chain tensioner to take up slack left when shifting to a smaller sprocket or chainring, a device to derail the chain from one sprocket onto another and a chain with sufficient lateral flexibility to run at an angle from the chainring across the various rear sprockets.

The most basic type of variable gearing involves fitting two different sized sprockets to a wheel to offer a choice of two gear ratios. The very earliest incarnation of this idea pre-dated the introduction of the freewheel in 1899 and comprised a single fixed sprocket on each side of the rear wheel, which had to be turned around to effect a change. It was not much more of a leap to double up the sprockets on the same side of the wheel and, from there, to put a pair of sprockets on each side to create the range of four gear ratios available to professional racers of the late 1920s.

The fundamental advantages of such a system over early examples of hub gearing are minimal power loss – the same as with a single freewheel – and the potential to provide a wide range of gears with acceptably low weight. The obvious problem with such an arrangement is that changing gear ratio requires at least a dismount and loosening of the wheel, if not wheel removal to turn it around. Another is that the range of gearing from highest to lowest is limited by the amount of rear wheel movement available to take up slack when the chain is run on the smallest sprocket.

Putting an idler or jockey wheel on an adjustable arm takes up chain slack nicely, leaving the inventor needing only to put all the sprockets on the same side of the wheel and to find a mechanism that will move the chain from one sprocket – or front chainwheel – to another while riding. The ban on variable gearing in the Tour imposed in 1919 by Frenchman Henri Desgrange exerted a powerful brake on technological development but did not entirely prevent it as racing cyclists and progressive tourists alike sought to improve on manual shifting and the hub gears available.

▼ Derailleur gears in a standard set up.

1. Cassette
2. Rear derailleur
3. Chain
4. Crankset
5. Front derailleur

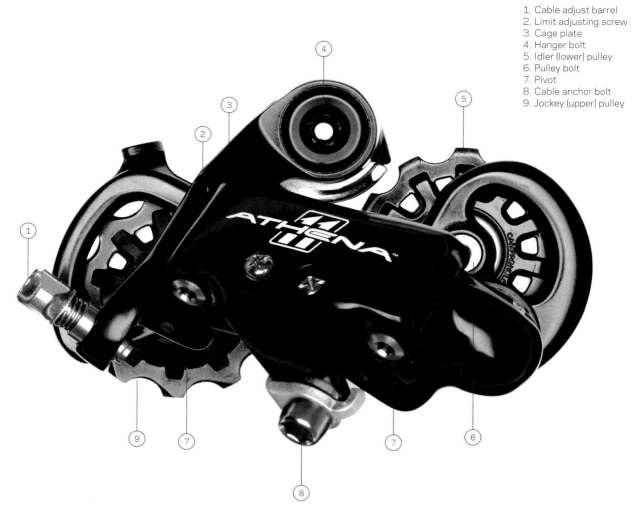

1. Cable adjust barrel
2. Limit adjusting screw
3. Cage plate
4. Hanger bolt
5. Idler (lower) pulley
6. Pulley bolt
7. Pivot
8. Cable anchor bolt
9. Jockey (upper) pulley

The first gears

True derailleur gears began to appear from the start of the 1920s but arguably the most significant early design was the 1928 Le Simplex model designed by French industrialist Lucien Juy. It used a spring-loaded short arm pivoting from beneath the rear dropout to tension the chain. This was moved sideways between two sprockets by means of a flanged wheel on a sliding rod, which was operated from a top-tube-mounted lever by a Bowden cable pulling on a small toggle chain of similar design to that on a hub gear.

Although the shift action was considered fast and accurate, the mechanism was exposed and vulnerable to damage in a fall. This was acknowledged in Simplex publicity of the day, which pointed out that in the event of damage the gear could be bypassed to leave a single-speed gear. The fragility of early derailleurs significantly delayed their general acceptance by the cycling public.

By 1933 the design worked across three sprockets but proved less popular for racing than a device known as the Osgear. Developed by retired Swiss racer Oscar Egg and more correctly called the Super Champion, the gear operated on the same principle as the original Vittoria Margherita; a long spring-loaded arm reaching backwards under the bottom bracket shell held a small idler wheel that maintained chain tension while underneath the chainstay a fork with tangs either side of the chain pushed it sideways when operated by a lever on the top tube. A thin protective disc prevented the chain from damaging the wheel spokes.

▶ The modern rear derailleur mechanism is unmistakable from any angle.

Back-pedalling

When the Tour de France permitted the reintroduction of variable gears in 1937, the Super Champion was the only type allowed in order to ensure that all competitors enjoyed equal machinery. In 1938, it was joined by the Vittoria Margherita. The Vittoria's earlier design employed a tensioning arm secured by hand using a ratchet quadrant and placed the actuating fork above the chainstay; not only did a shift require the tensioning arm to be released, but the rider was obliged to pedal backwards as the fork derailed the chain to another sprocket. The tensioning arm had then to be reapplied.

Although cumbersome to modern eyes, the Vittoria gear was highly successful in Italy. Its method of operation surely played a part in the conception of one of the most bizarre and yet revered derailleur mechanisms of them all. First known as the Cambio Campagnolo and originally introduced in 1933, the device that became the Tipo Paris–Roubaix also required a back-pedalling action to change gear.

Before this could be done, the rear hub itself had to be free to move in the rear dropouts, which was accomplished by a variation of Campagnolo's recently patented hub quick-release mechanism. The lever arm was at the end of an extended rod aligned with the right-hand seatstay, placing it within reach when riding. Once the hub was free to move backwards or forwards to provide or take up chain slack, the chain was then derailed by a fork above the chainstay actuated by a separate lever. A pinion on each end of the hub spindle engaged with a miniature-toothed rack on the underside of each rear dropout to maintain wheel alignment in the frame as the hub moved. Once the new gear had been engaged, the quick-release lever clamped the hub firmly and allowed pedalling to resume.

In the gear's final Tipo Paris–Roubaix incarnation, one lever performed both parts of the operation. Despite its apparent complexity, Campagnolo's extraordinary gear was successful. Italian Gino Bartali was said to be particularly fond of it and used it to win the 1948 Giro d'Italia. The single-lever version took its name from Fausto Coppi's dominant win in the 1951 Paris–Roubaix.

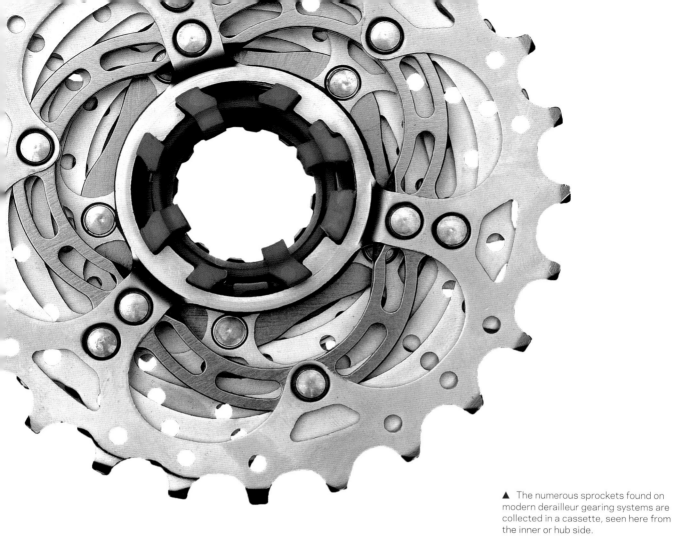

▲ The numerous sprockets found on modern derailleur gearing systems are collected in a cassette, seen here from the inner or hub side.

Development

Although they soldiered on into the 1960s, these and other racing derailleur mechanisms of the 1940s such as the Simplex Champion du Monde were rendered obsolete by Campagnolo's seminal Gran Sport design of 1951. It used a deformable parallelogram to provide the required lateral motion and employed 'throw' adjuster screws that determined the lateral range of movement. This made shifting into the highest or lowest gear quick and certain as the throw could be set to ensure the chain could not overshift.

Its twin jockey wheels, used to tension and guide the chain, also wrapped enough chain to make the double front chainring a practical proposition for racing. Double chainrings had been used since the end of the 1920s by cycle tourists, who had to shift the chain between rings by hand. By the mid-1930s, the Cyclo company offered a twin-plate cage changer, operated by rack and pinion, to work with a rear mechanism designed to wrap sufficient chain. The parallelogram mechanism proved effective as it could make the cage follow the angle from the small to the large ring and, by the 1970s, was the standard type in use.

With the Gran Sport, Campagnolo heralded an era of derailleur gears that were light, efficient and easy to set up and use. The deformable parallelogram forms the basis of all modern derailleur gears, or 'rear mechs'. Detail improvements to materials followed. Simplex offered mechanisms made in Delrin resin plastic that worked well but lacked durability; Huret offered numerous oddball designs popular with tourists and the cost-conscious and one model, the Jubilee, that remains one of the lightest rear mechs ever made. Campagnolo introduced lighter materials in place of the cast bronze of the Gran Sport to create the Record and Super Record gears.

With the Superbe, the Japanese SunTour firm brought the rear mech to more or less its current form. Its breakthrough was to realign the parallelogram, angling it from a short 'knuckle' arm with a slant that ensured the path of the jockey wheel cage followed the cone of the rear sprockets. The design was adopted by Shimano, who later added a sprung top pivot to make the mech wrap the chain closely around the sprockets in all gears, and is now near universal.

Rear mech design has improved since then, partly through the use of advanced materials such as carbon-fibre and forged light alloy and partly through appraisal of the detail operation of parts of the design. Fast, accurate shifting relies on both precise control of the jockey cage path and on the rigidity of the mech itself. Shimano's current front and rear mechs employ parallelogram plates shaped to maximise the stiffness of the assembly.

SRAM's RED 22 rear mech features a hollow titanium anchor bolt, part composites construction and carefully profiled teeth on the jockey wheels to reduce noise and drag. In recent years, the jockey wheels have been recognised as a potential source of energy loss; Shimano introduced 11-tooth wheels in 1997 in place of the previous 10-tooth standard and jockey wheels with as many as 15 teeth are now available from Berner-Bikes.

The larger the jockey wheel, the more slowly it rotates, reducing bearing drag, and the smaller the articulation angle of the chain as it runs onto the wheel. Adding both together, such wheels are claimed to save as much as 1.5W over the standard manufacturer's fitment.

SRAM's rear mechanisms feature a technology labelled Exact Actuation. The control wire runs onto an arc-shaped guide before being clamped. The angle of the wire relative to the clamp stays constant across the movement range of the parallelogram, so the amount of wire that must be pulled is the same for each gear shift. This ensures that shifting remains accurate across all the gears regardless of the axial placement of the mech relative to the sprockets.

The history of derailleur gearing is one of a constant struggle to refine what began as a brutal and unreliable concept. Today's derailleurs are anything but.

▼ Campagnolo's Super Record rear mechanism represents the high point in the development of early parallelogram derailleur technology.

Cassette

Before the cassette there was the multiple freewheel. Also known as a 'block' or 'cluster', it was the obvious solution to the derailleur gear's requirement for an array of rear drive sprockets. Adding an extra sprocket to a single freewheel created the first multiple freewheel and their number increased from two in the early 1920s to as many as seven by the 1980s, when the advent of the freehub (see pp. 80–81) heralded a new approach.

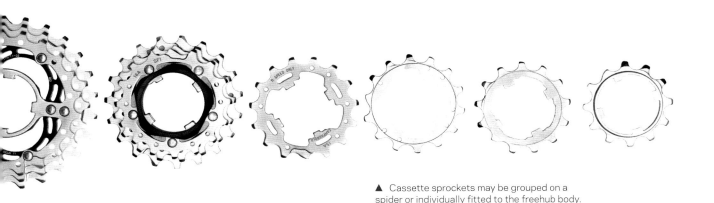

▲ Cassette sprockets may be grouped on a spider or individually fitted to the freehub body.

History

The multiple freewheel approach suffered a number of flaws: it was heavy, it made changing sprockets awkward and it was hard to seal effectively against water and grit. Removal was dependent on possession of a massive bench-mounted vice and, since the block's fine right-hand thread was tightened by pedalling, previous use by a powerful rider could make removal near impossible.

The Shimano Freehub and its associated collection of sprockets, collectively known as the cassette, made the cyclist's life a lot easier. Shimano's was not the first system to allow the easy removal of a multiple freewheel; that honour is usually accorded to Maillard's Helicomatic. It was, however, the first successful implementation of a freewheeling body forming an integral part of the hub and supporting splined sprockets.

The system is now almost universal on derailleur-equipped cycles. A modern cassette may contain from eight to 11 sprockets, each internally splined to fit the freehub body. There are two main spline patterns: Shimano and Campagnolo. Shimano's is by far the more common but almost all wheel manufacturers offer their wheelsets with a choice of Shimano- or Campagnolo-type freehub body. SRAM cassettes fit the Shimano spline pattern. Swiss manufacturer Edco has made a freehub body with a dual-spline pattern compatible with both Shimano- and Campagnolo-type cassettes.

In an effort to save weight by using aluminium for the freehub body, Shimano experimented in the mid 2000's with deep splines designed to spread the compressive load from pedalling force over a larger area. The easily recognisable, deep-spline freehub body is only compatible with a deep-spline cassette, although the deep-spline cassette will retro fit any Shimano-type freehub body.

► Multiple freewheel

1. Raceways on inner
   and outer ends
2. Ratcheted pawl
3. Heat-treated body
4. Sprocket teeth
5. Adjusting cone nut
6. Lock washer
7. Lock nut
8. Racing gear
9. Ball bearings

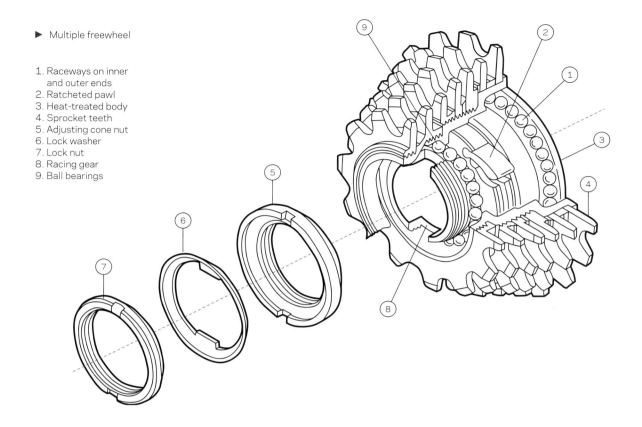

CASSETTE

The classic cassette comprises sprockets, spacers and a lockring and is often supplied assembled on a plastic splined dummy body, from which the cassette can be slid directly on to the matching splines of the freehub. Should a cassette be disassembled, it can only be replaced in one orientation with the freehub. This can be found by looking for the single narrow spline and using it as a guide to individual sprocket installation.

The sprocket teeth are given special ramps and indents that help the chain shift more quickly and under load. Campagnolo's version is called Ultra-Shift; SRAM favours OpenGlide while Shimano offers Hyperglide, which replaced the older and simpler Uniglide system in the 1980s. The spline pattern ensures that the shifting ramps of the various sprockets are always kept in correct relation to each other.

Sprockets and spacers may be presented separately, in groups of two or three on a light alloy spider or as a bundle usually riveted together complete with spacers. SRAM's RED cassette is machined from a single billet of steel and has an aluminium backing plate that transfers drive torque to the freehub body. Weighing less than a cassette composed of titanium sprockets,

the RED cassette offers superb performance but must be replaced complete should just one sprocket wear.

An internally splined lockring is used to retain the cassette. Again, Shimano and Campagnolo use slightly different patterns. The lockring is tightened against the outer sprocket, which has a serrated surface to grip the lockring and prevent loosening.

Shift Controls

Indexing – where each gear corresponds to a specific shift lever position – was a feature of the very first gear control levers, which were mounted on the top tube at a point reached by lowering the hand from the handlebars. Most hub gears such as those made by Sturmey-Archer are indexed, since it is not feasible to select a gear by 'feel'. However, cable-operated derailleur gears work happily without indexing and for the greater part of their history have employed a control lever held in place against the pull of the return spring by friction.

◄ Combining a brake lever with paddles that operate the derailleur gear mechanism, dual-control levers almost define the modern sporting road bike.

Dual-control levers

In its simplest form, this means the lever is equally resistant to movement in both directions and must, therefore, be significantly harder to move against the pull of the spring than with it. The considerable effort required can impair the precision needed to make a smooth, accurate shift.

One solution to this problem is a one-way clutch that disengages the friction element when the lever is moved against spring tension, greatly reducing the effort needed. The Simplex Retro-Friction and Sun Tour Powershift designs operated on this principle and were very highly regarded in their heyday during the late 1970s and early '80s. It is still used as a back-up in Shimano's indexed down tube and handlebar end shift levers, which are widely regarded as obsolete although they live on in the age of the dual control lever.

As their name suggests, dual-control levers operate both the brakes and the gear shift. The idea was first introduced by Shimano as part of the 1991 Dura-Ace groupset and labelled Shimano Total Integration (STI). It was swiftly followed by Campagnolo's Ergopower system, which was developed in collaboration with Sachs. Other attempts to make dual-control levers include an odd looking pair of levers by Modolo and variations on Shimano's theme by Microshift, but until the introduction of SRAM's DoubleTap system the Shimano and Campagnolo systems owned the market.

Shift mechanism

The shift mechanism of each system employs a pulley wheel to pull the inner cable and a ratchet system to hold the wheel in any one of its selected positions but all three differ in the way they are actuated; STI has a main lever that shifts the chain to a larger sprocket or chainring and doubles up as the brake lever and, behind it a release lever. ErgoPower's main lever operates only the brake; the secondary lever behind it shifts the chain to a larger sprocket and a small thumb lever on the inside of each hood releases the mechanism. SRAM's DoubleTap main lever operates only the brake, while the secondary lever behind it makes both the up- and down-shifts; one click releases the mechanism, while two clicks of the lever or more shift to a larger sprocket. In each case, the system is not 'indexed' per se, since the lever returns to a central position after each shift.

All three provide a fast and accurate shift and visually there is little to choose between them since Shimano found a way to hide the gear control cable under the handlebar tape while retaining STI's familiar functionality. Until the release of the 7900 Dura-Ace groupset, all STI levers had the cable running externally from the shift mechanism in the lever head to the down tube stop.

The external cabling provided a gently curved cable route that favoured smooth, easy shifting but came to be seen as retrograde with the arrival of SRAM's system, which like ErgoPower hides the gear cable. Hidden-cable STI shifts well but the levers, which contain an arrangement of interlocking prongs that carry movement at the lever to the shift mechanism inside the lever body, are bulky and cable-installation tricky.

So ergonomically efficient are dual control levers at gear shifting that few road cyclists would now care to be without them. Gear shifting can be as frequent as desired to let the cyclist ride at the optimal cadence whatever the conditions. This, even more than their ease and convenience, is what makes dual-control levers such a boon to cycling.

▼ Revealed; the intricacies of Campagnolo's nine-speed ErgoPower lever.

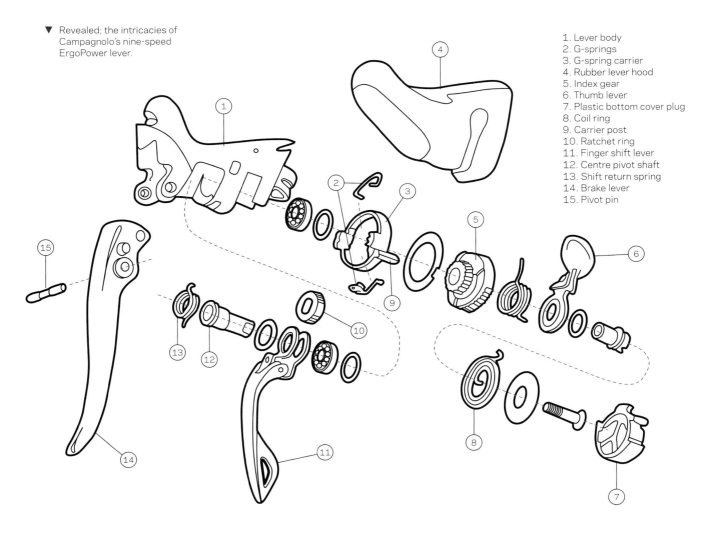

1. Lever body
2. G-springs
3. G-spring carrier
4. Rubber lever hood
5. Index gear
6. Thumb lever
7. Plastic bottom cover plug
8. Coil ring
9. Carrier post
10. Ratchet ring
11. Finger shift lever
12. Centre pivot shaft
13. Shift return spring
14. Brake lever
15. Pivot pin

Electronic Shifting

Quicker and more accurate shifts and reduced weight are just two of the benefits claimed for electronic derailleur shifting over cable or 'mechanical' operation. Another is surely the ownership of technology that makes the road bike more than simply human-powered, although the addition of complex, externally powered and potentially fragile componentry to the wonderfully simple and self-contained bicycle may not please everyone.

Form and function

Electronic shifting is now an established part of the road bike scene. The predecessor to Shimano's Di2 and Campagnolo's EPS electronic shifters, Mavic's ZMS system made its debut in 1993, a year after a prototype electronically controlled Mavic rear derailleur made a brief appearance at the Tour de France. Better known as Zap, the Zap Mavic System was generally well received and was raced by time trial stars such as Swiss cyclist Tony Rominger and British cyclist Chris Boardman, who rode it to win the 1993 Grand Prix Eddy Merckx.

Comprising a rear derailleur mechanism and a pair of 'strategically placed' control buttons on the handlebar, Zap proved unreliable and was shelved pending further developments. These arrived in 1999 in the shape of Mavic's Mektronic groupset. The ill-fated Mektronic comprised front and rear shift mechanisms, brake levers and a multi-function handlebar-mounted computer. The rear mech was powered by a small generator in the upper jockey wheel and operated by digitally coded radio waves sent by the computer.

Control buttons on the right-hand brake lever and hood combined with a third remote button to provide a multiplicity of shifting options. Shifting at the rear was exceptionally quick and possibly too much so as even the slightest touch on a control button would effect a gear change. The front mech was cable-operated by a thumb lever on the left-hand hood.

Mektronic had one flaw, which was unrelated to electronic shifting: the brake levers had a disadvantageous pull ratio and were moulded in flexible resin, leading to poor braking. Worse was to come with a decision by the Union Cycliste Internationale (UCI), cycle racing's governing body, to ban the components from competition after Mavic had tooled up for production. The brake hoods bore horn-shaped, inward facing projections that the UCI argued could provide an additional hand grip. Mavic later offered remodelled hoods but found few buyers outside France.

Development

The ease and speed of Mektronic's rear shift indicated that electronic shifting still had a promising future and, after much experimentation and testing, Shimano unwrapped the Dura-Ace 7970 Di2 (Digital Integrated Intelligence) groupset in 2009. Campagnolo was not far behind with a system that had been in development since 1992. The Italian firm provided several pro teams with fully

operational electronic shifting systems in 2011 and released the production EPS (Electronic Power Shift) components in 2012.

Both Di2 and EPS work well as might be expected of the two biggest companies in road bike component manufacture. In both cases, shifting is quick, reliable, trouble free and as near effortless as pressing a button can make it. Both feature flawless electronic front shifting that, in fact, works better than mechanical front shifting. The same could be said of their rear shifts, which readily change gear under high pedalling torque. Battery life is said to be excellent, with as many as 10,000 shifts available from a fully charged cell, although battery exhaustion is not unknown and will ruin a ride should it happen.

So important are electronic groupsets – both Shimano and Campagnolo are cascading the technology down through their ranges – that many manufacturers now offer frames specifically built for them. It is hard to argue that electronic shifting does not offer superior functionality and yet it has still to win over the entire professional peloton. Many leading riders prefer the informative tactile sensations of cable shifting to the feedback-light remoteness of changing gear through the medium of a push button, as do many leisure riders.

▼ Electronic shifting systems keep the number of major components to a minimum.

1. Rear mech
2. Battery
3. Connector
4. Lever controller
5. Computer

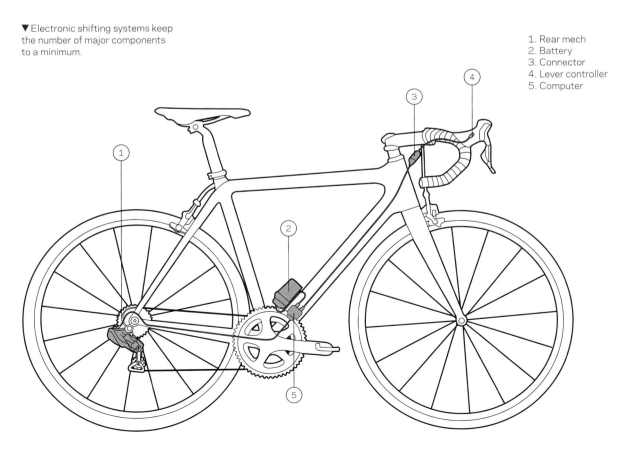

Hub Gears

Hub gearing places the mechanism providing the various ratios inside the hub of the rear wheel, where it is shielded from contamination by dirt and water and is less vulnerable to damage than a projecting derailleur mechanism. Its drawbacks include weight, slow and awkward wheel removal and relatively high power loss in most gear ratios.

History

It was perhaps only an accident of history that deprived the hub gear of pre-eminence in the world of performance cycling; riding a cycle equipped with a Sturmey-Archer three-speed hub, Lucien Petit-Breton was well placed towards the end of the 1913 Tour de France when he collided with a dog and was forced to retire. Petit-Breton, winner in 1907 and 1908, might well have won the Tour with a hub gear at a time when the derailleur gear was barely in its infancy and yet to be adopted by leading racing cyclists.

On the other hand, he might not have won. Contemporary accounts suggest that, despite being able to change gear while riding, he was unable to compete on the highest climbs with eventual winner Philippe Thys, who stuck with the then-standard technology of a rear hub with sprockets on both sides, turning the wheel around to make a gear shift. Maybe Petit-Breton simply wasn't as good a climber.

Despite the extra rear ratio offered by the Sturmey Archer hub, in 1914 most Tour participants were equipped with the well known Eadie two-speed hub, which had been introduced in 1900. This might have been the dawn of a glorious epoch of hub-gear dominance, but Tour organiser Henri Desgrange imposed a ban on variable gearing when the Tour restarted in 1919 after the First World War and so ensured that a three-speed hub gear would never win the world's greatest bike race.

▲ Hub gears can carry on working well after a century of regular use.

It wasn't the end of the hub gear's presence at the top of the road racing scene. By the late 1920s, the legendary Sachs Torpedo two-speed hub was a favourite of professional road racers, mainly because it saved the rider having to stop and turn the wheel to make a gear shift at a time when the alternative was a rear hub with sprockets on both sides. So important was the Torpedo hub to the European racing scene that the first three UCI world road race championships, in 1927, 1928 and 1929, were all won by riders equipped with it. The current Sturmey-Archer S2 Duomatic hub operates on the same principle, shifting sequentially between high and low gears with a simple back-pedalling movement.

By the 1930s, various derailleur gear mechanisms had been brought to a level of reliability that made them suitable for the demands of European professional racing and hub gears faded from the scene. In the UK, where road competition was limited to time trialling, hub gears were for the most part spurned in favour of a fixed-wheel transmission, which was considered more efficient. The famous Sturmey-Archer ASC close-ratio fixed-wheel hub was launched in 1948 in an attempt to attract British club riders but, despite being used in 1956 by Ray Booty to set a 'straight-out' 100-mile record of 3:28:40, made few inroads in a market that was turning to derailleur gears.

ROHLOFF SPEEDHUB

Hub gears remained popular with touring cyclists, who appreciated their reliability, until the 1950s. Later, they were primarily fitted to utility cycles; derailleur gearing offered a greater number and wider choice of ratios, making them superior not only for racing but for any field of performance road cycling. There the hub gear might still be were it not for the relatively recent development of hubs with ever more gear ratios, culminating in the wonderful Rohloff Speedhub.

Introduced in 1998, the Speedhub has 14 equally spaced ratios with each upshift increasing the gear by 13.6%. While expensive in comparison to competing derailleur systems, the Rohloff hub is robust and durable. With no vulnerable external components apart from the control cables, it is favoured by adventure touring cyclists such as former round-the-world record holder Mark Beaumont and is sturdy enough to be suitable for tandem use. Unfortunately it lacks a shifter suitable for fitment to dropped handlebars.

At a fraction of the price, Shimano's 11-speed Alfine hub has fewer gear ratios but is comparably free running and, like the Rohloff, available for use with disc brakes if desired. This and Shimano's eight-speed Alfine compete with multi-speed hubs from Sturmey-Archer and SRAM, ensuring that the hub gear remains a viable if under-appreciated option for the road cycling enthusiast.

▼ Rohloff Speedhub

1. Flange
2. Hub shell
3. Planet carrier
4. Planet wheels
5. Annulus
6. Sun wheels
7. Bearings
8. Sprocket
9. Spindle

◄ Shimano's Alfine 11 hub offers much of the performance of the Rohloff Speedhub at a fraction of the cost.

Form and function

With the exception of the NuVinci CVT hub and of a small number of early hub gears using a layshaft, hub gears employ an epicyclic or sun-and-planet gear train to effect a change of ratios. A series of 'planet' gear wheels, mounted in a plate, or carrier, engages with and rotates around a central gear wheel, the 'sun', which is rigidly fixed to the wheel spindle and therefore the cycle frame. Around the outside rotates a ring, or annulus, with matching gear teeth on its inside face that engage with those on the planets. The planet carrier rotates around the sun more lowly than the annulus.

With the rear sprocket connected via a clutch to the planet carrier and the hub shell to the annulus, the hub shell rotates more rapidly than the sprocket, creating an increase in gear ratio relative to the pedals. Connecting the annulus to the sprocket and the carrier to the hub shell does the opposite. In either gear, the spindle carries reverse torque and must be prevented from rotating backwards, usually be means of toothed washers or a torque arm. Connecting the hub to the sprocket bypasses the epicyclic gears and provides a direct drive.

In this arrangement, the gear ratio is calculated as the number of teeth on the sun plus the number of teeth on the annulus divided by the number of teeth on the annulus. Since the tooth count on the planets is irrelevant, they can be 'stepped' or given two different gear sizes on the same piece so the smaller gear runs on a larger sun than would be possible within a limited space. The tooth difference between sun and annulus is, therefore, smaller, providing closer gear ratios.

A hub may have more than one epicyclic gear train; some early three-speed designs used one for the low and one for the high gear, perhaps to avoid patent infringement as it uses two drives to do the work of one and adds unnecessary weight. An early Sturmey-Archer five-speed hub used two trains with different ratios to provide close and wide-ratio high and low gears. The direct drive middle gear was, of course, the same on both trains.

Carrying drive through a series of trains is used to provide a greater number of ratios. The Rohloff hub (see p. 119) employs three such trains with stepped planets and drive sequences chosen to give even percentage increases across the 14 ratios.

Performance

The most telling drawback of the hub gear is power loss in any gear that goes through the epicyclic train. This may be as much as 5% per train, or about 2% more than a well maintained derailleur gear, although the Rohloff hub, which uses roller bearings for the planet gears, is said to be around 98% efficient. Direct drive involves no power loss to the gears, making the hub gear arguably better than a derailleur in one of its gear ratios.

Hub gears tend to be heavy and bulky and can't be quickly removed from the cycle without disturbing control cables. With the exception of the Rohloff Speedhub, they are not compatible with quick-release skewers. On the other hand, the working parts are shielded from water and grit and need minimal maintenance in poor conditions. Performance does not deteriorate due to wear and the non-dished wheel is inherently stronger than a derailleur wheel.

Few performance cyclists will give the hub gear a second glance but those who do may find it a surprisingly effective solution to the search for a low-maintenance variable gear transmission.

Fixed-Wheel

Not to be confused with 'single-speed', a fixed-wheel
transmission employs a sprocket with no freewheel
mechanism. The pedals are, therefore, in a sense
attached or 'fixed' to the rear hub. The classic
arrangement is to screw the sprocket
onto the hub and then, if required, fit
a lock ring on a smaller left-hand
thread that prevents the sprocket from
loosening under back-pedalling pressure.

Gear ratio

Fixed-wheel transmission is the oldest and most basic type of chain-drive cycle transmission but one that retains a band of devoted adherents even in today's high-tech road cycling world and despite its adoption by trend-setting urban cyclists around the globe. Its essential simplicity and efficiency appeal to road cyclists looking for a more direct connection with the fundamentals of cycling and a fixed-wheel road bike set up correctly makes a rewarding, if demanding, riding companion.

The most important, and perhaps only important, decision to be made when riding fixed-wheel is choice of gear ratio. With no freewheel, the rider is obliged to pedal at a very high cadence downhill; the higher the gear, the lower the cadence. For general road use, the chosen ratio must be low enough for climbing, which means a gear that may feel too easy on the flat on a short ride. In practice, somewhere around 66in works well for most riders and will allow longer rides to be undertaken with confidence.

Many hubs built for fixed-wheel have a thread on each side, allowing the fitment of sprockets of different sizes. This two-gear system is a surprisingly practical arrangement that should not be dismissed as merely providing two equally unsuitable ratios. A practical arrangement that accounts for the needs of chain adjustment is to fit sprockets with a difference of two teeth, providing a lower gear for hilly terrain, a higher one for favourable conditions and both the motive and opportunity to practise rear-wheel removal.

The Sturmey-Archer S3X hub is fixed-wheel but not fixed-gear as it offers three gear ratios. The concept has obvious appeal but, in practice, lacks the purity and feedback of a single fixed sprocket; the hub is complex, heavy, less efficient in any but the direct-drive top gear and suffers from drive slack or backlash, so there is a brief lack of connection with the rear wheel as pressure is taken off the pedals. The hub works and has its advocates but offers a very different riding experience to a single fixed sprocket.

Correct chain tension is critical to safe and enjoyable fixed-wheel riding. If the chain is slack it may jump the rear sprocket at a high cadence and if it does will probably lock the rear wheel, causing a crash. The chain should be checked frequently and adjusted to give about 3mm of play at the tight spot.

'Single-speed' simply means that the cycle has only one gear ratio and the term may apply to a fixed-wheel or freewheel transmission. Perhaps the only comment that can be made in favour of the single freewheel for road cycling is that it makes life easier than fixed-wheel when riding downhill.

Gearing

British cyclists discuss gearing in inches using a method that dates back to the ordinary or penny-farthing bicycle, which had its front wheel driven directly by the pedals. The size of the cycle was determined by the diameter of the wheel, which was usually around 52in. Cyclists switching from the ordinary to the safety bicycle would compare the potential speed of the two by working out the effective diameter of the safety's driving wheel if it turned once per pedal revolution; a 26in-diameter wheel rotating twice per pedal revolution travelled as far per single pedal revolution as a 52in ordinary and so was geared to 52in. The Continental system involves calculating how far the cycle travels per pedal revolution and gives a figure 3.14159… times the British figure.

LOCK RING
In the UK, a fixed-wheel sprocket fitted with a lock ring counts as a rear brake and a cycle so-equipped needs only a front brake in addition in order to comply with the legal requirement for a working brake on each wheel.

◄ Sturmey-Archer's S3X three-speed fixed hub lacks a freewheel mechanism and is a valiant attempt to recreate a legendary hub of the 1950s.

5

Brakes

Disc brakes are becoming a more widely used fitment on lightweight road bikes. Their advantages over rim braking are subtle and come with drawbacks to match. Modern rim brakes are the result of a century of incremental development and work as well as narrow road bike tyres permit; they are far from obsolete.

Brake Evolution

A bewildering variety of braking systems has tempted the road cyclist over the decades, ranging from a simple pad or shoe pressed against the tyre through to today's sophisticated hydraulic-operated disc brakes. The themes of control, power and low weight have remained consistent, although the question of how much braking power is needed with lightweight road bike tyres is still far from being answered. In its latest form, the cable-operated rim brake offers all three along with the simplicity favoured by the purist and is far from obsolete.

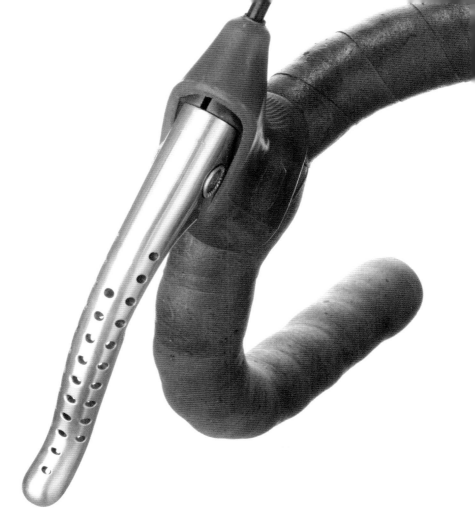

▶ Drop handlebar brake lever hoods designed to provide a comfortable hold became popular in the 1940s.

Early form

Bicycle braking began with a spoon pressed against the top of the front tyre – and moved swiftly on. No such device used with a pneumatic tyre could provide much retardation since the relatively soft tyre did not provide the compression resistance required. Tyres used on unmetalled roads would also acquire a lubricating layer of dust, further diminishing the braking effect. Worst of all, the brake wore out the tyre and heightened the risk of puncture at a time when tyres were expensive and punctures time consuming to repair.

None of this much mattered until the invention of the freewheel, since the braking on fixed-wheel machines was sufficient for the road conditions of the day. Freewheeling required another means of retardation and early cycle engineers looking for the most effective place to put a brake found it at the rim. The rolled-steel Westwood rims of the day were well suited to the application of braking force. The first truly effective rim brake was the Bowden Brake (see p. 138), which was designed by the inventor of the Bowden cable to take advantage of its ability to transmit force at a distance (see p. 130).

Susceptible to problems caused by improper installation, Ernest Bowden's brake was only moderately successful but his cable was a wonderful idea that spawned numerous inferior copies, each attempting to get around his patents by omitting some important detail such as the outer casing. The rash of breakages that followed affected the reputation of the Bowden cable itself and prompted the development of the road-actuated roller-lever brakes found even today on many utility roadsters.

Pulling outwards from the wheel centre against the underside of the rim, the roller-lever brake impeded wheel removal and was poorly adapted to competition use. Rod actuation was also heavy but it was reliable; the disastrous tendency of the soldered brass nipple of the time to pull away from the inner wire meant that, even in the 1920s, rod-operated pull-up centre-pull calipers remained popular with keen cyclists. Drum brakes offered an effective alternative that was especially welcome on the tandems of the day but their drawbacks (see p. 144) meant that they were rarely fitted to lightweight road bikes.

◄ The latest Dura-Ace brake caliper from Shimano adds a further pivot to the conventional dual-pivot layout – to great effect.

Caliper brakes

By the 1930s, cable-operated calipers designed to act against the almost vertical sides of the Endrick rim profile were commonplace. The placing of the blocks made wheel installation fast and simple and meant the caliper could apply a compressive force to each side of the rim rather than a pulling force against one face. The challenge now was to harness the rim's potential.

This was a decade of extraordinary inventiveness as a bewildering variety of cable-operated calipers arrived to tempt the keen road cyclist. The side-pull calipers that appeared after the First World War remained popular with professional racers but the lightweight and touring markets were filled with both side-pull and centre-pull designs of stamped sheet steel and, increasingly, forged light alloy manufacture. On the Continent, an early roller-cam brake known as the Jeay was highly regarded, while in the UK the Resilion design set new standards for power, if not for ease of installation.

By the 1950s, the lightweight road brake market was entirely populated by light alloy centre-pull and side-pull caliper designs, with centre-pulls considered to offer superior braking. Campagnolo's Record brake caliper, introduced in 1969 and featuring a lovely eccentric quick-release mechanism widely copied today, finally toppled the centre-pull from its perch and inaugurated a two-decade reign that ended with the advent of Shimano's 7400 Dura-Ace dual-pivot caliper. A series of centre-pull

'delta' brakes from Shimano, Campagnolo and Modolo had, in the meantime, come and gone having proven complex, hard to set up and, critically, lacking in power. Campagnolo's Delta brake design in particular was subject to harsh criticism for its atypically poor performance and is remembered best for its impressive appearance and flawless finish.

With the dual-pivot brake caliper, rim braking might have reached its zenith were it not for growing interest in mechanical linkages that enhance braking power and in hydraulic actuation (see pp. 136–137). Linkages such as the AeroLink used on SRAM's RED 22 and Bontrager's PowerAmp caliper employ complex geometries to increase the mechanical advantage of the brake lever through its travel and compete with dual-pivot geometry but at the cost of added complexity.

Hydraulic rim brakes present an exciting new direction for the basic arrangement that has stood road cycling in good stead for well over a century: obtain the maximum brake torque ratio by applying braking force to the furthest point from the hub possible.

Since that has always carried with it problems of heat management, rim wear and braking efficiency, the steady development of disc brakes offers an alternative route to the goal of powerful, dependable braking in all conditions. Discs may be the future, but rim brakes have much to offer.

Levers

Although cycle brakes are generally actuated by hand lever, inventors have tried several other arrangements including the back-pedalling coaster brake and even a twist grip that functioned like a reverse motorcycle throttle. Ultimately, hand levers have proven most suitable for performance cycling, offering as they do the optimum combination of fine control and power. The ergonomically effective dropped bar levers of today also offer an important hand position that was not widely available to enthusiast cyclists until the 1950s, although their precursors can be traced back to the first brake levers fitted to dropped handlebars (see p. 149).

With the introduction of cable-operated caliper brakes prior to the First World War, brake levers were placed at the front of the bend above the grips of bars that were gradually getting narrower and deeper but splayed out from the tops to the lower grips, providing two principal hand positions. The lever body, or 'perch', was small and unsuitable for holding. By the 1930s, the lever perch had become more of a hood, generally wrapped in cloth tape, but still small and, thanks to the projections of the fixing clamp, not yet designed to provide a comfortable grip.

True comfort arrived with the adoption by the 1950s of the internally tightened clamping band, which removed from the lever hood the uncomfortable projection previously needed for the clamp bolt. With the subsequent addition of the rubber hood, which removed the need for a cloth wrap, the essential format, if not shape, of the road brake lever had been set for the next 30 years.

Around the start of the 1980s, manufacturers began looking at ways to reduce air drag and one obvious candidate for improvement was cable routing. Hiding the brake cables under the handlebar tape saved in drag and was one of the first steps taken in improving cycle aerodynamics. Levers designed for the purpose were made by every major brake manufacturer including DiaCompe, Shimano, Campagnolo and Modolo. By now, the overall shape of the lever hoods was smaller, rounder and more comfortable than the substantial pistol-grip hoods of the 1950s and 1960s from firms such as Universal and Mafac.

The invention of dual-control levers added further impetus to efforts to improve lever and hood ergonomics, with small details such as the lever's pivot angle assuming considerable importance alongside the introduction of new rubber compounds and the gradual reshaping of the hoods themselves to create the examples of ergonomic excellence enjoyed by cyclists today.

Cables

The Bowden control cable is an extraordinarily useful invention. Patented in 1896, in its simplest form it comprises an outer casing and inner wire; the inner wire is free to slide within the casing and has a soft metal anchoring nipple at one end. In cycle construction, the other, 'free' end is simply clamped by the device to be operated.

Form and function

Cable is used to transmit a combination of pulling and pushing forces between components irrespective of their relative locations: the inner wire, which is strong in tension, pulls, while the outer casing pushes. The components connected by a Bowden cable must employ elements that can apply tensile and compressive forces: a brake caliper and its lever, for example, both have location points for the inner wire and casing, which also usually has an adjuster that effectively changes its length.

The casing is made of single-strand wire, usually steel, wound in a tight helix. Early casing used round wire but that of modern cables has a square section, as can be seen when cropping it, which is better at resisting compression. Bowden-type casing is covered in a protective plastic sheath that keeps out dirt and is manufactured with a Teflon or similar liner to reduce friction with the inner wire. This is made of multiple fine steel, usually stainless, strands and is either wound or braided; the latter is more flexible but not as strong.

Alternatives

For some automotive and similar flexible cable control applications, the inner wire may be replaced with a single thick wire stiff enough to apply compression. Although similar in construction, such cables do not operate on the original Bowden principle.

Although it is usual for the casing to be fixed at the 'master' end and for the inner wire to be fixed to moving elements at both ends, it is the relative movement of the wire and casing that generate pulling and pushing forces. It is possible to attach the wire to a fixed point and push against the casing to create the same effect: before the introduction of aero brake levers with concealed cable routing, some progressive cyclists tried for the same aero effect by inverting the cable run of old-style external-cable-route dropped bar brake levers so the nipple was held in the top of the lever body and the casing moved by the barrel in the lever that would normally have housed the nipple. The casing exited underneath and behind the lever and was looped back under the bar tape.

The arrangement's main drawback was the excessive cable friction caused by adding 180° of curvature to an inlined cable. The friction in a brake cable depends on the amount of curvature along its length, the coefficient of friction between the inner wire and its housing and the tension in the cable. The ideal straight line is impossible on a cycle but curvature should be kept as low as possible. Friction is greatly reduced by fitting a liner of some material such as Teflon inside the casing. Another improvement to cable-operated brake performance was the introduction by Shimano of a small return spring in the brake lever. This allows the spring in the brake caliper, which not only pulls the block away from the rim but pulls the lever back into place via the inner wire, to be made weaker. The friction the caliper spring generates within the cable is reduced by the same amount. The result is greatly reduced cable friction and increased braking power.

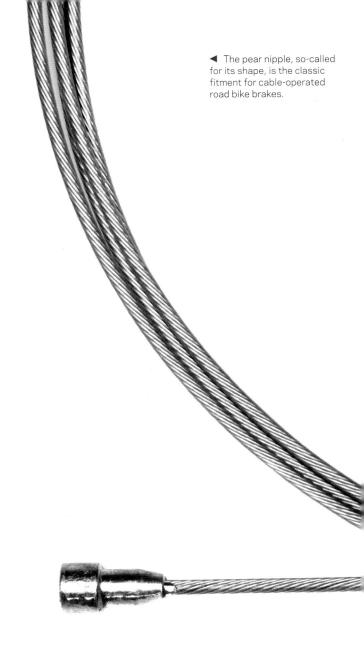

◀ The pear nipple, so-called for its shape, is the classic fitment for cable-operated road bike brakes.

BRAKE CASING

Two alternative types of casing merit mention: segmented and indexed gear. The segmented type exemplified by Nokon comprises short aluminium or carbon-fibre tubes with male and female spherical ends that slide over a liner to provide a flexible, incompressible tube that can adapt to tight curves without trying to spring back straight. Outer casing for indexed gears is designed to be extra stiff in compression and uses wires aligned in a shallow spiral bordering on parallel to the cable axis. Although stiff in compression, it is weak and must never be used as brake casing.

▶ Segmented brake casing

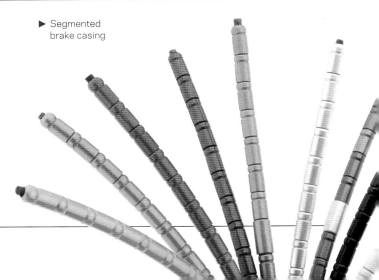

Side-Pull Brakes

Most cyclists would surely identify the side-pull caliper as the archetypical road bike brake. In its latest dual-pivot incarnation, it equips almost every complete off-the-peg road bike sold and the side-pull in one form or another has been the predominant road brake since the 1970s. It was also the first type of rim brake used in top level road racing, which gives it great pedigree.

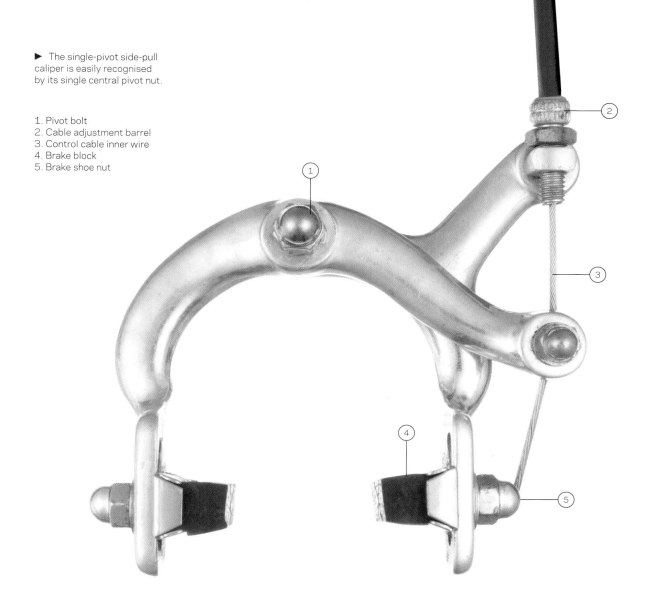

▶ The single-pivot side-pull caliper is easily recognised by its single central pivot nut.

1. Pivot bolt
2. Cable adjustment barrel
3. Control cable inner wire
4. Brake block
5. Brake shoe nut

Single-pivot

The side-pull is simply a brake caliper with its operating cable pulling on arms placed to the side of the brake. Almost all such brakes are designed as a self-contained assembly that needs simply bolting to the frame or fork. The fixing bolt is centrally placed and sits in a hole made for the purpose in the fork crown or stay bridge.

The caliper is secured using a nut; until the 1980s, this was situated on the outside of the fork crown or stay but to improve appearance and save weight by shortening the bolt, the nut, now a 'top hat' nut, now sits in a recess. This can create problems for those wishing to install a conventional mudguard; one inelegant answer is to place the mudguard main bracket in front of the fork crown.

In the classic single-pivot implementation, the bolt also forms the pivot for the arms and is provided with a nut and lock nut with which to adjust the free play in the arms. Behind the arms, a large-diameter boss locates the caliper return spring, which pushes both arms back from the rim. The spring should return both arms equally; if the blocks are not equidistant from the rim, the entire caliper can be rotated, usually using flats on the boss, to bring them into line.

Some older designs such as those by Swiss manufacturer Weinmann lacked any specific means of altering the brake alignment, which was instead accomplished by tapping one of the spring arms to drift the caliper around. Another method was to apply a spanner to both the front and rear nuts and apply torque in the same direction to each.

1. Caliper C-arm
2. Cable adjustment barrel
3. Quick-release lever
4. Brake block
5. Brake shoe nut

Dual-pivot caliper

Most dual-pivot calipers are provided with a small centring screw that moves both arms simultaneously, making them much easier to centre and keep centred than single-pivot calipers. There is also usually a spring tension screw that can be used to fine-tune the feel of the brake. The caliper itself has a Y-arm and C-arm on a short stub arm attached to the centre bolt. In standard practice, the Y-arm holds the right-hand brake block when looking at the caliper face-on. The stub arm is rigidly fixed to the centre bolt and sits in front of a mounting boss. One end of the caliper return spring is fixed to the stub arm while the other pushes on the Y-arm, forcing it back from the rim.

The Y-arm pivots on a bearing coaxial with the centre bolt. At the top of its upper strut sits the outer casing stop, complete with threaded cable adjuster. The C-arm pivots on a bearing at the far end of the stub arm and passes across the top of the wheel to provide a clamping location for the cable inner wire. Since the 1980s, higher quality brakes have used a small hex-headed screw to clamp the wire under a flat plate with a groove, avoiding the excessive crimping and weakening of the wire caused by the older, cheaper arrangement of passing it through an eye in a bolt and using a nut and washer to crush it.

Shimano and SRAM calipers have an eccentric-style quick-release mechanism at the end of the arm; ironically for the firm than invented the eccentric device, Campagnolo's quick-release comprises a small moveable peg in the brake lever that holds the lever in one of two positions.

Invented by GB brakes founder Gerry Burgess and first seen in the 1960s in the GB Syncron, the geometry of the dual-pivot caliper provides greater mechanical advantage over a single-pivot with the same 'reach'; the C-arm works like one arm of a centre-pull, so the distance from the pivot to the brake block is small and the lever arm long, maximising leverage. The Y-arm acts like the same component in a single-pivot caliper. It also has a projection on the opposite side of the pivot that presses downwards on the C-arm inboard of its pivot, moving the block away from the rim. The return spring therefore acts on both arms despite only pushing against one; the interaction of the two arms also ensures they move equal amounts as the brake is applied.

The classic dual-pivot concept has survived many attempts at improvement and is still the first choice for cable-operated road bike rim braking. Its excellent power and modulation carry over into the low-cost models from the major manufacturers, demonstrating the inherent 'rightness' of the original Syncron.

Campagnolo's more expensive road groups offer 'differentiated' braking through the use of a dual-pivot front caliper and single-pivot rear with the intention of providing greater power at the front, where it is needed, and improved modulation at the rear. In practice, the single pivot caliper is lighter, which is reason enough to use it where braking power is of lesser importance. The single-pivot type is also able to track a buckled wheel, as both arms can move sideways together around the centre bolt. A dual-pivot brake cannot do this and will move with the rim as a complete unit, loosening the attachment nut.

Stiffer and more effective than the single-pivot design, the dual-pivot side-pull is especially suitable for applications where a long-reach caliper is needed. 'Reach' is measured as the distance from the brake centre bolt axis to the middle of the rim braking track, which is also the middle of the blocks of any caliper that fits. Long-reach calipers obviously fit a frame and fork with greater clearance than short reach. Typical figures are 39–49mm for short reach and 47–57mm for long reach, implying that the slots in the arms provided for brake block vertical adjustment are 10mm long. This is not invariably the case and in case of doubt the reach of the cycle (or caliper) should be measured.

Brake blocks

Brake blocks for rim brakes may be a one-piece moulding with integral thread. More expensively, a replaceable block may sit in an aluminium or plastic shoe equipped with spherical washers that permit precise alignment of the blocks and rim. The shoe has an open end to allow removal of the block; the end must face backwards so that wheel rotation presses the block against the closed end of the housing slot, but in case a mechanic manages to install the shoe the wrong way around, most today have a small grub screw that engages with a trough in the back of the block to prevent its escape.

Removable blocks are available in a variety of compounds formulated to suit particular riding conditions. These may include wet and dry weather and, of course, extend to blocks made for riding in all conditions. Blocks are sometimes coloured to add visual appeal and for identification.

Carbon-fibre rims require carbon-specific brake blocks to ensure predictable braking. These may be of a special rubber compound that limits heat build-up or of cork, which has been found to provide excellent braking and a distinct aroma when used on a long descent.

▼ Brake blocks

Hydraulics

It was only a matter of time before road cycling's design engineers began to take a serious look at hydraulic brake operation. Its use in cycles dates back to the late 19th century. With the development of lightweight, expansion-resistant brake hose, it offers new possibilities for braking control and is being applied with success to both disc and rim brakes.

◄ Magura RT8
hydraulic rim caliper

Form and function

The virtues of hydraulic brakes are simplicity, reliability and effectiveness. It is simple because a 'closed' system, one that has no replenishing fluid reservoir, requires little more than a hose and a master and slave cylinder, reliable because, provided the fluid containment remains leak free, it does not become contaminated and effective because it allows pressure at the brake lever to be applied at a great distance without loss.

In operation, the fluid in a hydraulic system exerts pressure equally in all directions. The hose should be small in diameter, since bursting pressure is proportional to tube diameter, and of a rigid material to limit expansion, which would absorb some of the effort applied by the rider. Hydraulics permit a ready variation in the ratio of brake lever and brake pad pressure by playing with the relative diameters of the master and slave cylinders.

The master cylinder is operated by the brake lever and connected to the slave cylinder by the hose. Since fluid pressure is constant, the pressure on the pistons and therefore the force they exert is in relation to the ratio of their surface areas. If the master piston has an area of $10mm^2$ and the slave an area of $20mm^2$, a given force applied to the master will produce twice the force at the slave.

Since friction losses are non-existent and elastic losses minimal thanks to the rigidity of the hose and the incompressibility of the fluid, a hydraulic system can be set up with a relatively large slave piston area, allowing the designer to employ a higher force ratio and obtain greater braking performance than is possible with cable operation.

► The large-diameter disc and attendant caliper of a disc brake setup are an increasingly popular fitment on road bikes.

1. Hydraulic hose
2. Disc caliper
3. Disc
4. Disc carrier

Development

Magura made hydraulic rim brakes for dropped handlebars in the 1980s and '90s. Based on the German firm's HS11 mountain bike slave cylinder design, the HS66 remains one of the classic tandem rim brakes and is sorely missed. It was designed to be fitted to cantilever brake bosses and was operated by the same levers as the road bike-specific HS77, which featured unmistakable 'X'-shaped calipers.

Those Magura designs provided the excellent power and modulation for which hydraulic brakes are famed but failed to sell in quantity, probably because dual-control brake levers appeared at much the same time and offered greater functionality.

The latest wave of hydraulic road bike brakes is actuated by dual control levers. SRAM's hydraulic brake levers employ cable-operated DoubleTap shifting and offer a choice of disc or rim braking using an 'open' hydraulic system in which disc pad wear is taken up by piston movement, with the extra fluid needed being take from a reservoir at the master cylinder. The caliper rim brake

looks much like the firm's current RED22 cable-operated model and demonstrates that hydraulic actuation is at least as suitable for application to rim braking as to discs.

The disc system carries a weight penalty of around 450g compared with SRAM's cable-operated RED group while the hydraulic rim brake and levers add some 100g; cables still win where weight is an issue.

Shimano's R785 hydraulic system combines disc calipers and Di2 electronic shifting to avoid having to fit mechanical gear shifting and hydraulic brake operation components within the confined space of the brake lever housing.

Magura's RT8 hydraulic rim caliper is only currently available with time trial-specific brake levers, limiting its potential customer base, but demonstrates that hydraulic rim brakes have as big a future as hydraulic discs.

Brakes: Cantilever and Centre-Pull

The concept of the centre-pull brake followed naturally from the design of the original Bowden cable-operated brake, which employed a central rod or cable pulling equally on both sides of an inverted U-shaped stirrup, in turn pulling brake blocks against the rim. The classic centre-pull brake operates by pulling on the middle of a stirrup cable attached at its ends to roughly symmetrical arms, which pivot on spigots near the brake blocks and cross over at the cycle's centre line. The cantilever design is a particular type of centre-pull brake using lever arms angled outwards from their pivot points.

History

By the late 1920s, Bowden cable (see pp. 130–131) operation was the norm for lightweight road bike brakes and the best of them were of centre-pull design. While the long pressed-steel arms of early side-pull calipers lacked the rigidity required for powerful braking, the pivots of centre-pulls could be placed close to the blocks, making them short and stiff.

The most famous and highly regarded of them was the Resilion cantilever brake, which comprised a separate self-contained assembly on each fork of triangulated stamped steel arms either side of the leg bolted to a long shoe. The main bracket was made in a number of shapes for attachment to fork blades of various profiles. The two cables ran to a junction box and were from there pulled by a single cable from the lever.

Braking power was exceptional and the Resilion remained a popular fitment on tandems until the 1950s. Its main drawback stemmed from the very rigidity of the fixture, which did not permit the brake blocks to follow a severely buckled wheel rim. Also lacking a quick-release mechanism, the Resilion fell out of use with the post-war development of effective side-pull calipers.

The cantilever principle, however, lived on in two of the most famous cycle brake designs ever. Both were from Mafac of France and used the bare straddle wire with which cantilevers are associated.

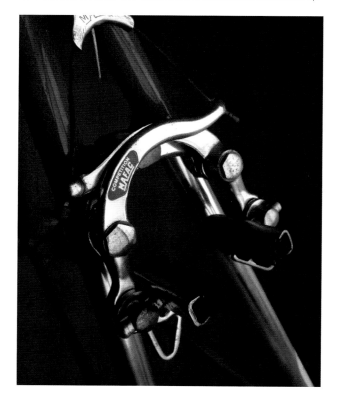

▼ The classic centre-pull brake was made by French firm Mafac and is notable for its wrap-over arms and short straddle wire with stirrup.

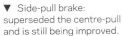

▼ Side-pull brake:
superseded the centre-pull
and is still being improved.

▼ Centre-pull brake:
tricky to set up but has
performed well enough.

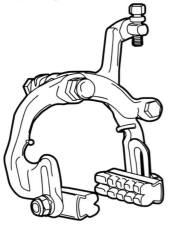

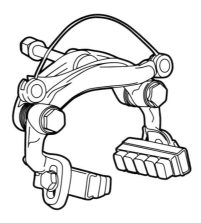

Mafac cantilever

The legendary Mafac cantilever dates from 1948 and, in various versions, proved popular for four decades with tourists, tandemists and cyclo-cross riders. It requires mounting bosses brazed to the fork legs and stays and a stop, or hanger, for the main cable outer casing but offers powerful braking and the huge clearance needed for off-road riding. The Mafac cantilever is one of the most influential designs in cycling history, providing the inspiration for the first generation of mountain bike brakes and the brazed-on boss fixture to which they and V-brakes are attached.

Mafac's Racer may not have had the same influence, but it was used by a generation of racing cyclists of all abilities and was widely copied. Instead of brazed-on bosses, the brake requires a standard central mounting hole of the sort suitable for a side-pull caliper. The arms, which cross over above the wheel to keep the brake profile narrow, pivot at the ends of a short beam that is bolted to the fork crown or seatstays.

Like the cantilever, it requires a hanger for the brake outer casing. On some machines built for centre-pull brakes, the hanger is brazed to the seatstays but positioning the hanger for the front brake has always taxed the ingenuity of cycle mechanics. For most of the 1950s and '60s, the Mafac Racer was the pre-eminent brake in the professional peloton and, despite being widely copied, was never equalled.

It not only provided the best braking performance of the era but was versatile, with blocks that could be adjusted for height and for angle in two planes.

As side-pull caliper design improved, the centre-pull brake lost ground and, by the 1970s, was used only on lower-cost sports and touring bikes. Like the cantilever, it was finicky to install with multiple adjustments available and two cables to clamp on each brake. Many cyclists who have struggled with a pair of 9mm spanners and a recalcitrant straddle wire stirrup will wonder why centre-pulls lasted as long as they did.

The 'low-profile' cantilever, which differs in arm geometry from the Mafac design, was used on mountain bikes until the introduction of the V-brake and is easier to install thanks to detail refinements and an improved straddle wire design. New versions of the Mafac brake remain a favourite of cyclo-cross riders and convincing copies of the originals are made by Paul of the US. They look great – and they work.

Linear-Pull Brakes

Although primarily associated with mountain and utility bikes, linear-pull or V-brakes are a feature of the latest generation of 'aero' performance road bikes such as LOOK's 695 Aerolight and have a further use in road bike construction as an alternative to cantilevers for touring and cyclo-cross-based machines. They offer simplicity of installation and adjustment and are powerful and easy to modulate but require a suitably constructed frame and fork.

Form and function

A regular linear-pull, or as it is commonly known, 'V', brake – V-Brake is a Shimano trademark – comprises an arm on each side of the wheel pivoting at the lower end on a boss of the same type and position as used for cantilever brakes. Each arm's pivot is equipped with a return spring and screw adjuster to permit the blocks to be centred equidistant from the rim.

With one or two exceptions, dropped handlebar brake levers are not designed to work with full length V-brakes, as the cable pull ratio is wrong. With V-brakes, the ratio of length of inner wire pulled to brake block travel is the same as the ratio of the distances from the pivot of the brake block and the cable anchor point. Dropped bar levers only pull about 12mm of inner wire in total and most of the lever travel is taken up in pulling the brake block up against the rim, leaving little left before the lever hits the handlebar.

One solution is to fit a pull converter such as the Travel Agent, which alters the pull ratio to suit; the other is to fit 'mini' linear-pull brakes, which have shorter arms and therefore require less cable to be pulled to bring the blocks into rim contact.

Whereas the brake blocks of flat-handebar, linear-pull brakes sit about one third of the way up from the pivot, those of mini 'v's sit a little less than halfway between the pivot and cable housing. Ideally, the arms of V-brakes for use with road levers should be around 85mm long. Brake shoes usually have a post and spherical washer fixing that permits accurate block alignment with the rim.

The left arm has a stirrup strap for the noodle pipe, which forms the end of the outer casing and curves through either 90° or 130° to align the inner wire with the clamp on the opposing arm. As there is no intervening straddle wire, linear-pull brakes are sometimes known as direct-pull. A slot in the noodle pipe housing allows it to be unshipped to open the brake block for rapid wheel installation.

The direct cable route and straight-line pull minimise friction and cable flex and, combined with the short, rigid connection between the blocks and arm pivots, provide exceptionally smooth and controllable braking. The layout also has a narrow frontal profile that fits within the silhouette of most front forks. A popular use is to fit a mini linear-pull brake behind the fork blades of a time trial machine, hiding the arms from air flow. The route of the noodle pipe provides the necessary clearance with the down tube when the handlebars are turned.

LINEAR-PULL DEVELOPMENT

This idea has been taken further by manufacturers including LOOK and Ridley, whose Noah FAST's F-Brake concept uses faired-in short-arm linear-pull brakes that, when the brake is idle, form a part of the outside surface of the fork. Instead of a mechanical pivot, the arms are part of the fork or stay's carbon-fibre moulding and rely on the material's elasticity, flexing at their base as the arms are pulled inwards.

Besides improving aerodynamics, the use of mini V-brakes in this way saves weight. Although the best mini V-brakes, by firms such as TRP, are exceptionally light, the braze-on steel bosses required add significant weight. This is less of a problem for touring cyclists looking for the clearance to fit fatter tyres, for whom the mini V-brake is the solution to the problems posed by the complexity of cantilever brakes.

▼ Linear-pull brake

1. Boot
2. Brake cable anchor bolt
3. Mounting bolt
4. Spring tension centring screw
5. Arm
6. Noodle holder (quick release)
7. Noodle
8. Blocks

Disc Brakes

Disc brakes offer many theoretical advantages over brakes that operate on the rim of the wheel and are already fitted across a significant portion of the high-performance road bike market just a few years after their introduction. The most significant advantage enjoyed by disc brakes is that they avoid the various disadvantages of rim braking.

Form and function

Bicycle brakes use friction to convert the kinetic energy of the cycle and rider into thermal energy, or heat. A rim brake heats the blocks and the rim; if the rim stays hot for long enough, it will heat the air inside the tyre, causing it to expand enough to either blow a clincher tyre off the rim or melt the glue of a tubular tyre.

If the rim is dented, a rim brake won't work well and may not be useable at all. Debris trapped in brake blocks gradually wears away the rim's braking surface, leading to a dangerous condition unless the rim is replaced before it cracks. Discs avoid all these problems and are easily replaced when worn. Furthermore, the rims of lightweight road bikes are made of materials that are less than ideal for use as braking surfaces and may therefore generate less friction than the materials used in discs.

Against this, disc brakes require a wheel with tangent spoking to resist braking torque and a strong mount for the caliper. Not only do they add weight, but they affect the resilience of the cycle and, in particular, the fork, which must have blades suitably beefed-up for the purpose. The weight of a disc-equipped bike is around 1kg greater than a comparable rim-braked machine.

◀ The surface of a brake disc quickly becomes marked with characteristic score lines where it is worn by the pads.

Operation is simple: rigidly fixed to the wheel hub, the rotating disc is gripped between pads housed in a caliper attached to the frame or fork, generating friction and converting the kinetic energy of the cycle and rider into heat, or thermal energy. The caliper can be actuated by hydraulic pressure or by Bowden cable. Cable-operated, or 'mechanical', disc calipers suitable for use on road bikes are widely available. They require less cable pull (see V-brakes pp. 140–141) than flat-bar brake levers and will therefore work with dropped-handlebar brake levers.

Mechanical calipers are relatively heavy; the cable inner wire pulls a lever that rotates a sturdy ball-and-ramp mechanism to apply pressure, usually to just one of the pads; the thin disc flexes and is pushed against the fixed opposing pad. A screw adjuster compensates for pad wear and must be used whenever lever travel becomes excessive.

A hydraulic caliper employs one or more slave pistons (see p. 136) to apply pressure to the pads: a single piston presses on one pad, as with the mechanical caliper, while the more effective opposed piston design does as the name suggests and uses a piston on each pad to press both against the sides of the disc simultaneously. An 'open' hydraulic system automatically compensates for wear by drawing more fluid from a replenishing reservoir as the pads become thinner and the pistons move closer together.

Development

The hybrid TRP HY/RD caliper arguably offers the best of both worlds, using a cable from the brake lever to actuate a self-contained hydraulic caliper; the small arm presses on a master piston that in turn moves slave pistons to push the pads.

Unlike a drum brake, a disc is easily cooled by airflow, limiting heat build up. Some calipers or pads are fitted with fins that further aid heat dissipation. Wheels with discs are also easier and quicker to remove and replace than with drums. On the other hand, discs can still become very hot with consequent brake fade and leading manufacturers are making great effort to combat this. Shimano's Ice Disc has a three-ply construction of aluminium with a stainless steel cladding to provide both thermal transfer and a hard-wearing braking surface; excess heat is not an issue.

DISC BRAKE IN OPERATION

Fluid pressurised by the master cylinder pushes against the slave cylinder piston or pistons. A hydraulic disc caliper employs one or more pistons to apply pressure to the pads; a single piston presses on one pad, as shown; in cycling applications, the thin disc is usually flexed sideways by the piston-operated pad against the static pad in the caliper. The more effective opposed-piston design uses a piston on each pad to press both against the sides of the disc simultaneously.

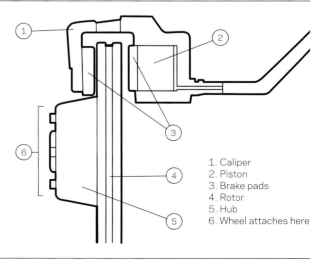

1. Caliper
2. Piston
3. Brake pads
4. Rotor
5. Hub
6. Wheel attaches here

Drum Brakes

Rarely seen on performance road bikes but used for decades as a drag brake for tandems and as a low-maintenance option for utility cycling, drum brakes answer – and pose – many of the same questions as disc brakes.

▶ The workings of a drum brake are neatly hidden from view and the elements inside a bulge in the hub barrel.

Types

The mechanism of a conventional cycle drum brake is relatively simple (see p. 145). An integral part of the hub is the drum's perimeter and it provides a large flange for spoke location, which also creates a torsionally stiff wheel provided it is laced with tangent spokes. Most such cycle hubs are sufficiently rigid to stay round when subjected to uneven spoke tension.

Shimano's Inter-M Roller Brake is a self-contained component that is attached to the hub via splines; it employs three steel shoes forced outwards against the inside of the drum by six rollers on ramped beds and must be kept lubricated by grease to prevent seizure.

Performance

The main advantages of the drum brake are consistency and durability. The braking surfaces are kept away from contamination inside a shielded space and, since the friction material and drum can be made of heavy duty materials, maintenance requirements are minimal.

The brake obviously works independently of the wheel rim, which does not suffer wear and can be damaged without affecting brake operation.

Braking power is generally good. No doubt had drum brakes received the development that has gone into discs and rim brakes it would be better still. It is sufficient to make the most highly regarded hub brake ever made arguably the best choice still for a tandem drag brake despite the recent development of discs said to be suitable for the task. The Arai Drum, which is threaded onto a hub, has been out of production for some time and now commands a high price when examples come up for sale. This brake won't stop a laden tandem in a hurry but is an effective drag brake – kept applied on a descent to prevent speed build-up – as it has a large cast-alloy drum with vanes to keep it from overheating.

Excessive heat build-up can afflict the drum brake, which is why Shimano's Inter-M device is not recommended for tandem use. More important from the perspective of performance cycling are its weight and the time taken to remove and replace a wheel with a drum. As with performance, these are two aspects of the design that could surely be improved with thought and the use of lightweight materials; quick-release drums were once fitted to competition off-road motorcycles.

As with disc brakes, the drum layout puts weight where it is least welcome, especially at the front of the cycle. A heavy hub adds what is known as 'unsprung weight' in other fields of transport. This lessens the suspension effect of a resilient fork blade. The provision of a reaction arm also impairs ride comfort as the fork must be more heavily built to accommodate the forces applied to it.

Ultimately, the performance of rim brakes throughout the history of the lightweight road bike has been seen as good enough to make the weight and complexity of the drum brake an unnecessary addition to the cycle. It is, however, a viable alternative to the disc where minimal maintenance requirements take precedence over all other considerations.

▲ Shimano's Inter-M drum brake features cooling fins cast as part of a disc, making it easily recognised – or confused with a disc brake.

DRUM BRAKE IN OPERATION

Twin curved shoes, each faced with a friction lining, are forced against the inside surface of the drum by a lever-operated cam. The lever sits on the outside of the brake back plate and is actuated by cable. The shoes are attached to the inside of the back plate, which tries to turn under braking force and must be rigidly anchored to the fork or stays by either a reaction arm, or strut, or pegs.

▼ A drum brake's workings are simple, effective and reliable.

1. Brakeplate lever
2. Brakeplate
3. Return spring
4. Cam
5. Brake shoe lining
6. Braking surface
7. Wheel spindle
8. Hub shell
9. Brake shoes
10. Fulcrum
11. Anchor

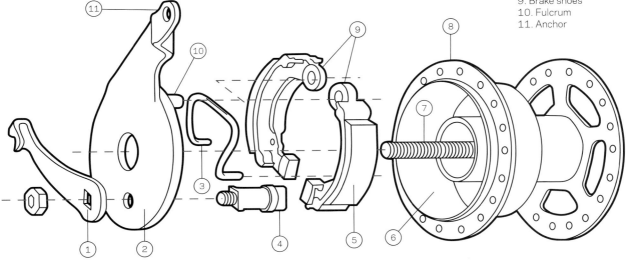

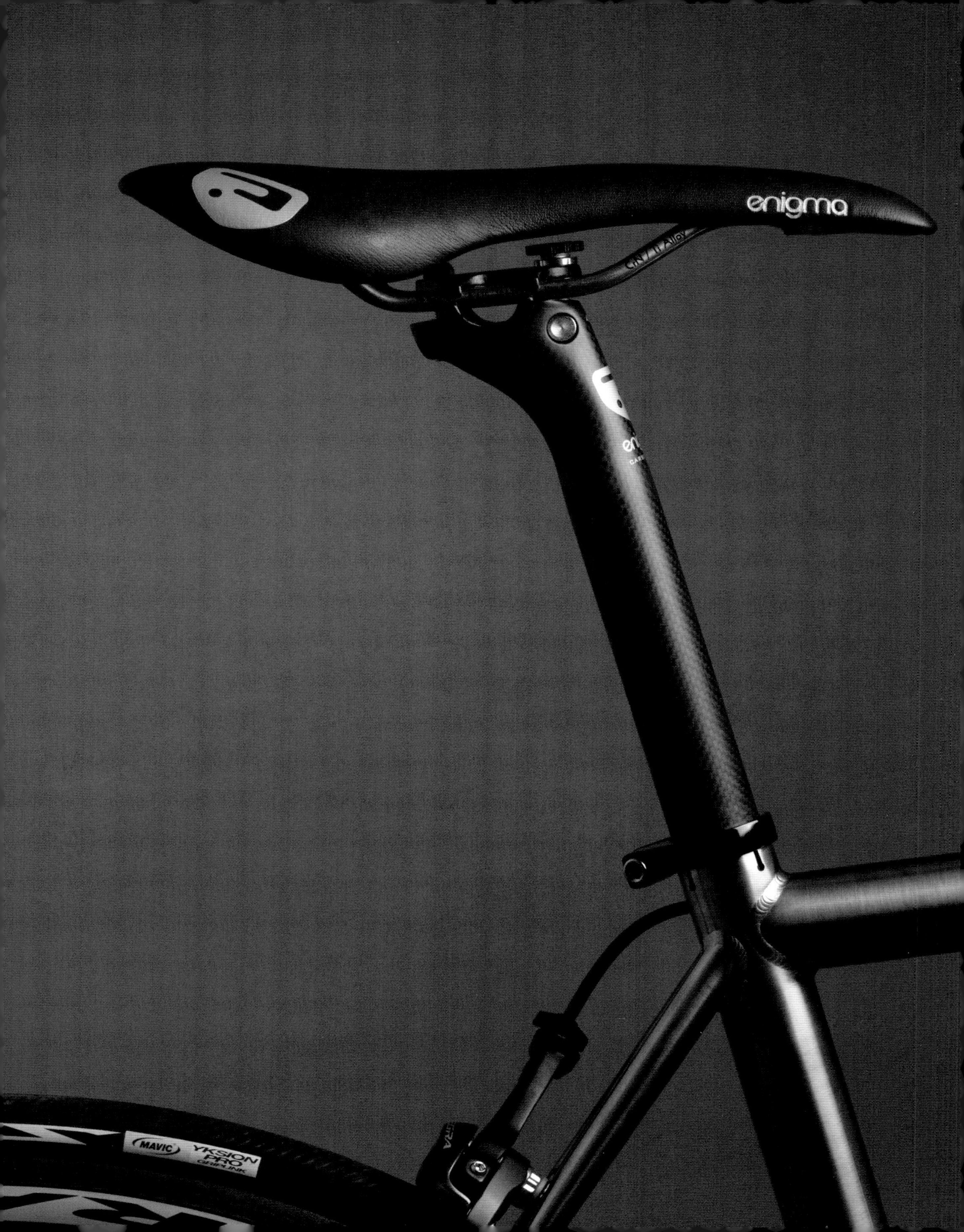
enigma
MAVIC
YKSION
PRO

6

Contact Points

The popularity of comfortable
leather saddles can mean only
one thing: while some progress
has been made in saddle design
and manufacture, the industry
has yet to find the perfect solution
to the most persistent problem in
cycling. At least handlebars and
stems are better than ever, or at
least lighter and stiffer. Can the
same be said of seat posts?

Handlebars

Whereas flat handlebars are little more than a convenient place to position the brake levers, rest the hands and apply steering forces to the cycle, the dropped handlebars that are the mark of the road bike are a masterpiece of functional ergonomics.

▼ Soft tape may be
wrapped around dropped
handlebars to provide a
comfortable grip in any
hand position.

History

The shape of handlebars offers more than a choice of hand
positions and, therefore, trunk angle. The importance of
this angle to long-distance road riding comfort should not
be underestimated: the shape and placement of the brake
lever hoods not only puts them within easy reach from the
handlebar tops and contributes to relaxed handling in a
group but provides handholds at the ideal grip angle when
riding out of the saddle.

Dropped handlebars have, of course, long been associated
with cycle racing and the adoption of a wind-cheating
crouch is a prerequisite of speed on a bike. As with so many
components on a road bike, the early development of drop
handlebar shape was driven by the demands of racing. It
was also heavily influenced by advances in brake technology.

The handlebars used by racers of the 'Heroic Era' at the
end of the 1890s were wide to provide plenty of steering
leverage over the rough roads of the time and placed the
grips barely below the saddle. Cable-operated caliper
brakes arrived prior to the First World War. Their levers
were placed above the grips of bars that were gradually
getting narrower and deeper. The lever body, or 'perch',
was small and unsuitable for holding and the bars splayed
out from the tops to the lower grips, providing two
principal hand positions. British riders could choose from a
wide range of handlebar bends including the fabled North
Road and the Marsh, which was a time triallist's favourite.

The development by the early 1950s of the rounded
aluminium lever body with rubber hood and hidden clamp
combined with vertical drop handlebars to provide a
recognisably modern arrangement. Aluminium handlebars
of Duralumin alloy made their appearance in the late 1930s
and were made in a variety of bends such as the famous
AVA Randonneur, which slopes upwards away from the
stem before commencing the drops. Nevertheless, steel,
which is more resistant to gouging, cracking and fatigue,
remained the preferred material for top level racing
handlebars until the early '60s, when Cinelli's beautifully
crafted light alloy products set a new industry standard.

Featuring a central sleeve that minimised the effect of
superficial damage on the bars' integrity, Cinelli handlebars
were expensive and bought only by the most serious and
well-heeled of road cyclists. More affordable aluminium
bars and stems were offered by firms such as GB, Atax,
Ambrosio and Philippe and were made in numerous
shapes and widths.

By the 1970s, Tecno Tubo Torino (3T) and Italmanubri
(ITM) were making racing bars and stems the equal of
those by Cinelli. These three firms dominated racing for
several decades until the high point of the traditional quill
stem and road handlebar combo at the end of the 1990s.
Nor were they notably conservative; Cinelli's Spinaci
mini-handlebar concept, mimicked by ITM and 3T, pushed
the boundaries of handlebar ergonomics until banned by
cycle racing's governing body, the UCI. The same firm's
Ram design integrates the bars and stem in a one-piece
carbon-fibre moulding of undoubted visual appeal.

Development

Increasing worldwide interest in cycle racing at the close of the 20th century boosted the industry and competition between the many newer brand names in handlebar manufacture such as Deda, Profile, Pro, 3T, Zipp and USE has resulted in an explosion of choice over bar shape, size and material. Carbon-fibre, for some time the preserve of small-scale makes such as Ax-Lightness of Germany, is now in widespread use but has yet to prove significantly superior to the finest aluminium handlebars. The use of advanced aluminium alloys, heat treatment and metal manipulation have allowed manufacturers to create exotically curved bars of astonishingly low weight and impressive stiffness.

Construction

A typical current performance road handlebar in aluminium or carbon-fibre has a pronounced, oversized centre bulge of 31.7mm diameter in place of the 26.0mm bulge or sleeve used on the classic Italian bars of the 1960s onwards. Oversizing adds strength and stiffness and allows the use of thinner tube walls without sacrificing either. The larger bar circumference also provides the stem clamp with a greater surface area.

At the front and rear of the bars, either side of the bulge, is a groove. The brake and gear cables fit snugly in the grooves under the handlebar tape to create a slim, comfortable hand hold and appearance.

From the flats the bars curve forward before starting their downward path. From this point, they may be given a form designed to provide a more comfortable hand hold or may continue with a regular curve and round cross section to the drops themselves. The bend may be a traditional continuous curve or 'anatomic', with a reverse kink that fits the palm of the hand.

Size variations include handlebar width, depth of drop and reach from the bulge to the brake lever mounting point. A shallower bend provides less of a difference between riding positions on the hoods and drops such bars are popular with women and with men wanting a less extreme crouch to go with a comfortable reach on the tops.

▶ The oversized bulge at the handlebar centre point adds strength and stiffness where needed as well as increasing the surface area available for clamping.

◀ EVA foam provides endless opportunities to add decorative touches.

Comfort

Many means of improving comfort have been tried over time and all have their modern counterpart. The most obvious is to provide some sort of cushioning between the hard, rounded surface of the handlebar and the palm of the hand. Tape wrapped around the bars is the road bike's signature.

Cloth tape is the antique choice. Each successive layer of multiple wrappings of cloth tape adds a surprising degree of softness but wrapping thin cloth tape over foam rubber padding is more effective and was popular with racing cyclists and tourists until the arrival in 1987 of Cinelli's Cork Ribbon. Made by blending small fragments of cork with expanded EVA foam, it still offers effective cushioning and attractive looks. Its shock absorbing properties can be further enhanced by laying a strip of the tape along the upper surfaces of the bars before wrapping the tape.

Cork Ribbon quickly consigned shock absorbing wraps such as Spenco grips to the bin and many versions of Cork Ribbon are now available. Alternatives such as Fizik Microtex and Lizard Skin rarely offer as much comfort but tend to be more resistant to abrasion. Leather tape, introduced some five years ago by leather saddle specialist Brooks and now available from other sources, offers an unusual tactile sensation and lacks shock absorption but is popular as a complement to a leather saddle. Any 'retro' air it gives a bike is spurious; true retro requires cloth tape.

▶ Leather handlebar tape, here by Brooks of England, adds a touch of luxury to the right type of machine.

WRAPPING HANDLEBAR TAPE

Well-wrapped handlebar tape is the finishing touch for any performance road bike. For a bike to look good, the bars need to look good.

Wrapping bar tape is essentially a straightforward job that requires some dexterity but no special tools or previous experience. There are a couple of details to get right for a professional finish.

First is the direction of wrap. There are four ways to wrap a side: starting from top or bottom and spiralling in either direction. Beginning the wrap from the stem bulge gives a neat finish to the stem end of the tape but has a major drawback; the overlap means the rider's hands will tend to roll back the edge of the tape when riding.

Start from the bottom to avoid this and take care to achieve symmetry by winding the tape so that the two sides are angled opposite ways. There are two options: wind outwards under or over the bar from the bottom. Some sources insist one of these is better since it prevents the tape being pulled loose but, in practice, this does not happen with well-tensioned tape.

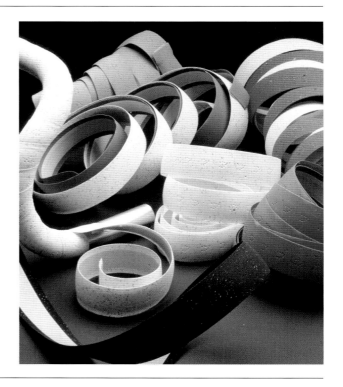

Stems

Connecting the handlebars and fork steerer, the stem is a highly
stressed and safety-critical component. It must resist bending and
torsional loads, hold the handlebars securely and provide a flex-free
interface with the fork. Road stems today are one of two types:
the quill, which has a long neck that fits snugly inside a threaded
steerer tube and the threadless, engineered to work with a threadless
headset. The threadless system is a recent development that has
replaced the quill stem in high-performance road bike construction.

History

Early stems were of brazed steel construction and, designed principally to provide a secure mount for the handlebars, lacked much of an extension. The requirements of sports riding and competition prompted the development of stems with extensions that placed the bars further forward. The Major Taylor stem, named after the cycling champion of the 1890s, was adjustable and featured a handlebar clamp that could be slid along the extension tube to find the required length.

A non-adjustable stem of the correct length is much lighter. Stem length increased as frames became smaller and lighter and reached a recognisably modern form by the 1930s. Various designs were tried including the curved 'Swan Neck', but for performance riding the pattern comprised a tubular extension brazed at one end to the bar clamp and, at the other, to a lug also holding the stem neck.

Aluminium stems of the 1930s were usually styled to look much like the steel stems of the day but with a separate quill stem, or 'expander tube', pressed into a one-piece cast extension and clamp. The extension was often decorated with exaggerated lug 'profiles' cast into the metal. French touring cycle builder René Herse crafted his unique lightweight stem extension from solid billet aluminium to leave two parallel arms with a large gap. Here again, the quill was pressed into place.

The urge to decorate aluminium stems with imitation lugwork survived until the 1950s and the switch to one-piece forged aluminium construction but such fakery lived on and could be seen on an AVA model of the 1970s nicknamed the 'Death Stem' for its tendency to crack at the top of the spreader slot, with disastrous results.

Some time before then, stem design had moved on. Cinelli of Italy's fillet-brazed, chrome-plated steel stems are perhaps the most beautiful ever made but surely the most admired stem in road cycling history was the Milan firm's 1A model, which was introduced in 1963. This iconic

> ▶ Cinelli's 1R quill handlebar stem offered a sleeker look but never gained the following of the 1A that preceded it.

component, which graced the professional peloton through the era of Eddy Merckx, is so revered that Cinelli recommenced manufacture in 2011. Of one-piece forged aluminium alloy construction, it has a 'milky' anodised finish and is secured using an expander cone. On later examples this was pulled by a long internal hex head bolt. Handlebar clamp diameter is 26.4mm and the stem should only be used with suitable Cinelli road handlebars. Its successor, the 1R stem, did away with the underslung handlebar clamp in favour of an internal wedge pressed against the back of the handlebar by a hidden bolt. Although visually clean, the 1R never achieved the status of the 1A thanks, perhaps, to its tendency to creak loudly at the wedge.

Stems similarly styled and constructed were made by firms such as 3T, ITM and SR. The quill stem's apogee was reached with the Cinelli Grammo, which was of welded titanium construction. TIG-welded steel stems enjoyed a brief period of popularity in the late 1990s and models such as the ITM Eclypse weighed as little as 260g for a 100mm extension.

The quill stem

The quill offers one or two advantages over the threadless system: handlebar height adjustment is easy and does not disturb the headset, the quill can be made in any practicable length, allowing for the bars to be raised to a considerable height, and quill stems offer a slender, lightweight appearance favoured by some cyclists.

Adjustment is easy. Once placed at the desired height, the stem is locked in place by a nut at the bottom of the quill. Older stems have a conical nut and a spreader slot cut along the quill. As the nut is pulled upwards by the stem bolt, it spreads the end of the stem to jam it against the inside of the steerer. This inevitably distorts and stresses the quill at the start of the slot, with risk of fracture, and applies a ring of pressure at some point on the steerer, which, if the bolt is over-tightened may bulge, become work-hardened and crack.

To loosen the conical nut, the end of the stem bolt is tapped sharply. This requires a tool that may not be available on the road. More recent quill stems rely on a wedge nut, which also jams the quill against the steerer but without distorting the quill. It applies force over a wider area and can be loosened by slackening the stem bolt.

▼ Carbon-fibre cladding can be used to enhance the visual appeal of an aluminium handlebar stem.

Threadless

The threadless stem is, in effect, simply an extension clamped to the outside of the steerer tube, which extends above the top of the headset (see pp. 46–47). It can be moved along the steerer to permit height adjustment by adding or subtracting spacers of appropriate thickness.

Current designs owe their shape and use of materials to advances in manufacturing techniques, stress analysis and, of course, experience gained over the decade and more since they first appeared on road bikes. The steerer clamp bolts, for example, are now almost invariably found at the rear of the stem. While less aesthetically pleasing than it might be, this maximises the stiffness of the extension. Some early designs placed the steerer clamp split on one side of the extension, putting the bolts where they are under additional stress when the handlebars are twisted.

Torsional rigidity, an often overlooked but vital aspect of stem performance, is where the threadless stem generally excels. An early example that did not was Cinelli's Sesamo, which comprised two extension halves split horizontally along the stem centre line. It was held together by a number of small bolts and clamped the steerer and bars firmly when tested in the vertical plane, but proved entirely lacking in torsional rigidity as could be demonstrated by twisting the handlebars.

CENTRAL BULGE

To ensure a safe and secure assembly and avoid overstressing the stem, the bar clamp's inner diameter must be a precise match for the handlebars' central bulge. Although mountain bike and old steel handlebars have a 1in (25.4mm) bulge, the high-performance aluminium dropped bars made from the 1960s by Italian firms traditionally use a fatter bulge diameter of 26.4mm for Cinelli and 25.8mm for 3T and ITM. Over the last few years, the 1⅛in (31.8mm) oversized format has become the de facto standard for high-end road bikes.

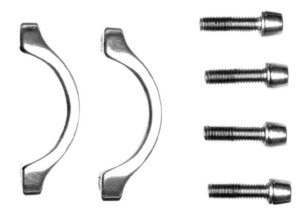

A typical high-performance road stem today is manufactured using net forging technology to form a one-piece tubular aluminium extension with precisely controlled internal and external dimensions. Two hex bolts clamp the steerer tube while four are used to pull a face plate against the handlebar, securing it to the extension. Similar designs can be CNC-machined from billet aluminium.

This arrangement makes for a stem that can weigh as little as 100g for a 100mm extension. As ever, there is room for variation in face plate and bar clamp design; the bolts may be wide-set or placed close together or the plate may be split into two half-collars. The Spanish firm Rotor employs face plate with just two bolts but each with a dual thread pitch design that generates immense clamping force.

Carbon-fibre is increasingly used for stem construction, sometimes as an outer layer bonded to a net-forged aluminium core. This manufacturing technique, sometimes described as 'choc-ice', adds little to stem strength or stiffness and such stems generally weigh as much as directly comparable all-aluminium examples.

All-carbon construction of the type exemplified by French manufacturer TIME's beautiful Monolink Ulteam offers potential improvements in stiffness and weight but, at 135g for a 90mm example, shows the difficulty of improving on the weight of the best all-aluminium designs.

▼ The threadless stem's top cap with central bolt provides a quick and effective means of adjusting headset-bearing free play. It also provides a highly visible branding opportunity.

Saddles

Widely reputed amongst non-cyclists to be one of the most vicious instruments of torture not invented by the Spanish Inquisition, the road bike saddle is, in fact, as perfectly adapted to its task as human ingenuity can make it. It must seat the rider in comfort and provide a stable pedalling platform that does not interfere with leg movement. The key to ensuring both is to find a saddle that fits correctly.

History

For just less than a century, cycle saddle design and construction followed the template established by Brooks of England in 1866, in which a piece of thick 'butt' leather moulded to shape is riveted to an adjustable frame. At the rear, a curved cantle plate the width of the saddle supports the leather upper; the front is fixed to a narrow curved nose plate. Steel wire rails connect the two plates via a threaded device that allows the nose to be pushed forward and tension the upper by taking up any slack or sag.

Brooks held a patent on their tensioning device and built an enduring reputation for making high quality saddles that kept their shape for longer than any other. Even Brooks saddles, however, are vulnerable to the main drawback of the leather cycle saddle; it does not like getting wet. To shape the upper it is soaked in water and then pressed around a former before being dried out. Soaking it again returns the leather to its soft, easily flexed and mouldable state. If ridden like that, it can stretch irretrievably and ruin a carefully acquired shape that suits the owner.

Such were the trials of leather saddle ownership that the multi-spring saddle with waterproofed fabric upper was a popular fitment on roadsters and sports cycles both before and after the Second World War. While needing little care or maintenance, such saddles were too heavy and uncomfortable to challenge the legendary Brooks B17 and its peers for serious performance cycling.

Given its importance to rider performance and its working conditions, a leather racing saddle was a rider's most prized possession, but also a high maintenance item that needed almost constant care and attention. Although something easier to care for was needed, leather remained the material of choice for racing saddles until 1959 and the unveiling of the moulded nylon plastic UnicaNitor saddle. The upper sat on flat-sided steel rails that required a special micro-adjustable seatpost. Not only was the saddle weatherproof, but including seatpost it was some 70g lighter than the equivalent Ideale saddle with its heavy fixing clip but without post.

The French national team used the saddle for the Giro d'Italia and Tour de France but, despite its low weight and imperviousness to weather, it didn't prosper. It was slippery and uncomfortable thanks to its unyielding material and the complete lack of ventilation through the unperforated nylon upper. Ventilation holes and a grippier dimpled finish did nothing to improve matters and by the mid-1960s it was rarely seen beyond the school bike shed.

British road racing star Tom Simpson successfully attached a layer of leather to the plastic shell, prompting Cinelli to offer in 1970 a version of the Unica saddle with a thin layer of foam under a leather covering. Now durable, lightweight and comfortable enough for racing, the saddle established the pattern for almost every racing saddle that came after.

▲ The extensive Brooks leather saddle range includes a 'pre-softened' series of models recognisable by a brown finish and supple, pliant leather upper from new.

During the 1980s, road saddle design progressed rapidly thanks to manufacturers such as Selle Italia, IscaSelle and San Marco. Selle Italia's Bernard Hinault Turbo remains, along with San Marco's Concor, one of the iconic designs of the decade. Both looked dated next to Selle Italia's dainty Flite, which was the prettiest model of the 1990s. Those who tried the Flite and found it wanting were spoilt for choice by models such as San Marco's Regal and Selle Italia's Turbomatic, the favourite of both Miguel Indurain and Jan Ullrich.

Attempts around the end of the '90s to alleviate the supposed problem of penile numbness resulted in a wave of saddles with holes of various shapes intended to reduce pressure on delicate perineal tissues. By the early 2000s, saddle manufacturers were dreaming up ever more imaginative, performance enhancing features; the then-fledgling firm of Fizik's Arione was not only 30mm longer at the back than most of the competition, apparently to offer an extra seating position, but had flexible sidewalls designed to permit easier thigh movement.

The most notable trend of the last couple of years has been the reissue by several respected manufacturers of models discontinued a few years ago such as the Turbomatic and Flite. San Marco's Regal remains popular with discerning cyclists wanting comfort the equal of that provided by a Brooks, suggesting saddle design reached some kind of peak in the late '90s.

▼ The sleek lines of a lightweight synthetic racing saddle may or may not indicate a comfortable riding experience.

Saddle rails

One constant in cycle design is the desire to save weight. The growing use of carbon-fibre has brought the weight of the very lightest mainstream saddles such as the Selle Italia SLR Tekno to below 100g by ditching padding and a leather or similar cover and using carbon-fibre rails.

Rail design and layout is proving a rich seam to mine by engineers looking for new solutions. Y-shaped wishbone rails and rails moulded into the sides of the upper offer potential weight savings, as do saddles using a non-standard connection with a dedicated post as exemplified by Selle Italia's Monolink design.

Pressure relieving holes in the saddle upper remain popular, as do attempts to rethink the whole idea of the cycle saddle by using materials in an unusual way such as weaving the upper from interwoven fibres. Saddles with a split nose and no nose have been tried with debatable success. The search for the perfect road bike saddle continues.

The conventional lightweight saddle's shaped upper is firmly but not necessarily rigidly fixed to twin rails spaced to fit a standard seatpost. The rails are usually 7mm deep but can be 10mm deep to add strength, especially if made in carbon-fibre. Titanium and tubular steel are the two preferred options for mid-weight saddles. Shock absorbing dampers may be fitted at the rail's insertion points to isolate the upper from vibration.

The rails have a straight section that permits the saddle to be slid through the seatpost cradle. There is no standard for orientation of the straight section with the upper; if the saddle cannot be placed as desired on a standard seatpost, one with a different layback can be fitted.

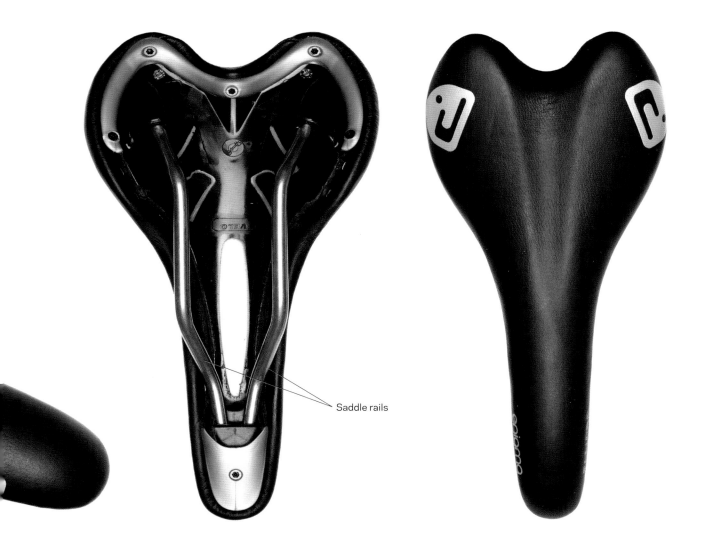

Saddle rails

Saddle shape

The upper's nose must be narrow enough to permit free leg movement. Attempts to build saddles without a nose invariably suffer from the fact that it contributes to machine control, obliging the rider to use body weight to influence steering. Traditional design considerations give the nose deep sidewalls, which allow the thighs to slide up and down them. Saddles such as Fizik's Arione, which have a shallow nose with low sidewalls, can rub the inner thigh and, if nothing else, damage the fabric of shorts or tights.

The rear of the saddle upper is shaped to support the sit bones, or ischial tuberosities, which project downwards from the middle of the pelvis. Saddles of various widths designed to match the disposition of the sit bones have proven successful at reducing saddle pain as they place the saddle's cushioning precisely where it is needed. A foam pressure gauge is used by the retailer to measure the distance apart of the sit bones. A typical range of saddles will offer three widths.

Saddle angle should be set with care as it has a major role in determining ride comfort. The angle should be chosen to ensure that the pelvis remains stable during pedalling; the sit bones should rest on the 'meat' of the padding and there should be no tendency to slide forwards or back. In general, a saddle set level with the ground or very slightly nose-up will answer these requirements. Penile numbness or compression of the perineal tissues is often caused by forward rotation of the pelvis; a nose-up saddle can help combat this by promoting a rearward position on the saddle. Ultimately, fine-tuning saddle angle must be at the rider's discretion.

▲ A pronounced sag in the middle of the saddle upper is popular with some riders and the source of intense dislike for others.

BROOKS SADDLES

Despite their reputation for blissful riding comfort once 'broken in', Brooks saddles are widely supposed to be miserably uncomfortable for the first few hundred miles of riding. This is, in fact, a myth; 'break-in' is both quick and simple. The saddle must simply be ridden for as little as 160km (100 miles), ideally on one long ride when still new.

The rider's sit bones press on and flex the saddle upper, quickly degrading the adhesion between the elastic collagen fibres of the leather and the hard glue-like substance that joins them, leaving the fibres free to move and absorb the vibrations from the road surface. Angling a Brooks saddle distinctly nose-up for the duration of the break-in will make the process faster by keeping the sit bones in the right place.

Brooks 'Proofide' treatment applied thickly to the underside of the saddle and worked in with a warm thumb will protect from stray water splash. An occasional application of Proofide to the top surface will keep the leather from drying out and cracking. Otherwise, these saddles will last for decades with minimal attention. Saddle life can be extended by resisting the temptation to tension the upper unless absolutely necessary.

Seatposts

Of the many integrated saddle clamp seatpost designs
made since Campagnolo introduced the classic twin-bolt
Gran Sport model in 1958, few have been as effective
at doing what a seatpost should do, which is to hold the
saddle securely, in the right place and at precisely
the desired angle. It is a surprisingly challenging brief.

History

The seatpost arrived with the invention of the safety bicycle. The seat-to-crank axle dimension of the ordinary bicycle was fixed by the size of the driving wheel, which was always as large as the rider's legs would permit.

No longer limited by wheel diameter, the frame of the safety could be made to accommodate a wide variety of leg lengths by simply fitting the saddle to a tube or post telescoping inside the frame. The extra-shallow seat angle of most bicycles made until the end of the 1920s required a post with forward extension so the saddle could be placed just behind the bottom bracket axle. This was abandoned in favour of a plain post as angles became steeper.

On both types, a heavy steel clip arrangement comprising various radially grooved washers and plates shaped to fit the rails holds the saddle. The end of the clip fits over a smaller-diameter neck at the top of the post and nuts on the ends of a through-bolt clamp the whole affair together. The grooves are needed to ensure that the saddle does not start to tilt as the rider's weight bears on it. This usually acts at a point behind the clamp, forcing the saddle to tilt backwards if the clip is loose. The grooves lock the clip but the angle between them limits the precision possible when levelling the saddle, which may end up with its nose either slightly higher or lower than desired.

In place of the clip, Campagnolo forged at the end of the post an integral projection, or head, which on each side supports a rail cradle free to rotate around a spigot. The saddle rails are clamped to the cradles by two cross beams, one in front of and one behind the cradle axis. By tightening the bolt holding the rear beam and slacking the other, the saddle can be tilted backwards with practically infinite precision – and vice versa.

Once tight, the bolts stay tight and there is no tendency for the saddle to tilt. The post's main drawback is the difficulty of reaching the forward bolt head, which sits under the middle of the saddle. Campagnolo provided a 'cranked' spanner for the purpose that few riders carried while riding.

Although the design, quickly followed up by the lighter Record seatpost in 1960, rendered the plain post with clip obsolete, the expense of the integral post ensured that the earlier device soldiered on in lower-cost road bikes until well into the 1980s. With the post with clip now only found on low-cost utility cycles, the integrated post is the road bike industry standard.

Road bike design has also benefitted from the development for mountain bike use of posts longer than the 200mm or so from the 1980s and before. As posts have lengthened they have become more flexible, with commensurate improvements in ride comfort.

► An angled slot is often employed in a seat tube clamp used with a carbon-fibre seat post in order to spread the clamping stresses and minimise the risk of damage to the post.

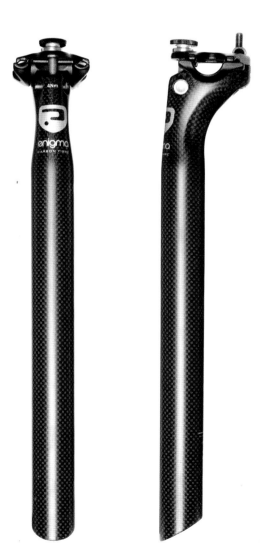

Seat angle

Seatposts generally bear at least two marked pieces of information: the shaft diameter and the minimum safe insertion level, which should not be ignored. Seatpost diameter varies in increments of 0.2mm; 27.2mm is the most common in a range that can run from 25.0mm to a fat 31.6mm depending on manufacturer.

Seatposts drilled to save weight enjoyed a boom in popularity in the 1970s but suffered the major drawback of letting water enter the seat tube. Fluting can be used to lighten a post with thick shaft walls. Better is to use a shaft with thinner tube walls in the first place; not only should the post be lighter, but the flutes limit lower height adjustment.

Most seatposts work best when used with standard 7mm diameter round-section saddle rails; some won't work at all with the deeper oval rails seen on many super-light saddles. 'Layback' is the distance between the post's shaft centreline and the centre of the rail support cradle. Road bike posts typically have about 25mm of layback; a straight post has none.

The seat angle is a function of femur length and saddle height. Most riders have a femur length in proportion to height that means, with normal length cranks, the resulting frame seat angle will be 73° from horizontal.

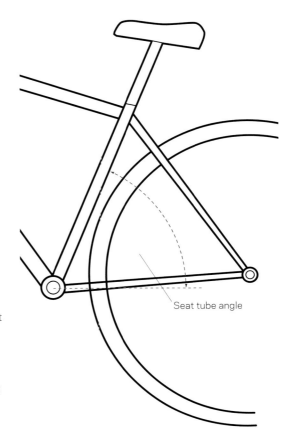

Seat tube angle

Integrated posts

Reliability, difficulty of adjustment and micro-adjustability are features common to virtually all integrated seatpost clamps with twin bolts placed fore and aft.

The awkward bolt placement of most twin-bolt layouts has encouraged manufacturers to find a single-bolt system that works. To prevent slippage these rely either on friction or on a serrated cradle which meshes with the support in a series of positions determined, as in the separate clip design, by the angle between teeth. In this respect, a cradle moving around a flatter arc, as in Shimano's late-model design, offers smaller angle changes per tooth.

Many single-bolt posts rely on friction and, therefore, a substantial bolt to prevent movement. The 1970s Campagnolo Super Record post is a typical example. The cradle moves on a smallish, radius arced support with friction between the contact faces of the support and cradle preventing movement when tight. A fine M8x1 thread allowed the clamp to be done up very tightly indeed, but other, similar designs using a cheaper M8x1.25 bolt could prove slip-prone.

Innovation abounds in integrated post clamp design as manufacturers look for the perfect setup. 3T's DiffLock uses two concentric splined barrels with differentially

spaced splines to provide 0.5° increments of saddle angle adjustment. Slippage is eliminated, but at the cost of fiddly adjustment.

Variations on the micro-adjustable twin-bolt system are popular. It is used for the excellent Thomson design from the US, which employs a couple of other noteworthy features. Each post is machined from extruded 7000-series aluminium alloy of a profile big enough to provide material for the cradle support. The tube bore is of elliptical section with the deeper sidewalls orientated fore-and-aft to resist the bending loads applied by the rider's weight. The post shaft is CNC-machined to size and, where layback is required, bent backwards a little way below the clamp. If Thomson posts want anything, it is, perhaps, a sleeker clamp.

Although carbon-fibre is making inroads, aluminium is easily the most popular material for seatpost manufacture; an aluminium integral shaft and head formed as one piece is acceptably light and aluminium can be extruded and is easy to machine and manipulate.

A thin-walled aluminium shaft flexes enough to provide a little shock absorption. Titanium has been employed to the same end by manufacturers large and small from Campagnolo to PMP.

'Aero' seatposts have a teardrop-section shaft that is considered to lessen air drag. The shape makes the post very stiff where flex is desirable. A partially aero post designed to fit a round section seat tube reduces the length available for adjustment and stresses the post at the junction with the seat lug. Any aero advantage is likely to be of little use outside of competition.

Recent trends include leveraging the flexibility of carbon-fibre to improve ride comfort. Canyon's Vertical Comfort Lateral Stiffness (VCLS) 2.0 post is perhaps the most ingenious example yet.

MAINTENANCE

Seatpost maintenance mostly concerns corrosion prevention. In some conditions an aluminium post will corrode readily if housed in a steel, titanium or carbon-fibre frame. The aluminium oxide formed occupies more space than the plain metal, effectively expanding to press against the inside of the seat tube with sufficient force to jam the post completely. As always, prevention is better than an attempt at a cure.

Coating the inside of the seat tube with grease or, better, a corrosion inhibitor, will prevent the galvanic corrosion that causes the problem. This should be done wherever dissimilar materials are in contact. Care should be taken to avoid excessive force when clamping a carbon-fibre post. Using a particle-filled carbon grip compound may prevent slippage. A regular creak heard when pedalling can often be traced to corrosion between the saddle rails and seatpost clamp.

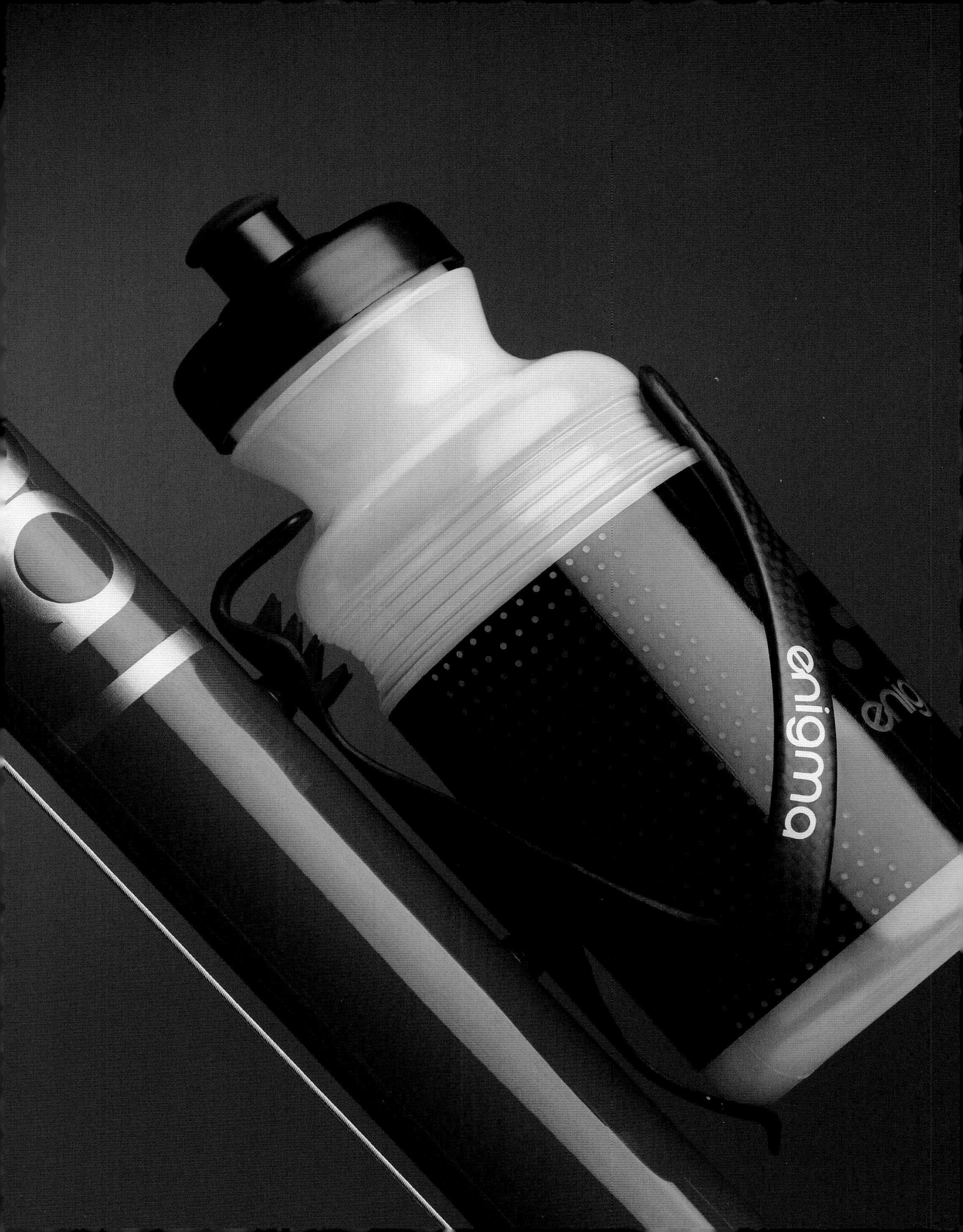
enigma

7

Accessories

If rarely needed, accessories complete the road bike's assemblage and ensure that every ride is as pleasurable as it can be. The range of products available not only ensures that no need is left unanswered but provides plenty of opportunity for personal expression; some cyclists like to carry everything their cycle will transport while others won't even take a pump and inner tube – let alone two tubes.

Cycle Computers

The desire to know how far and how fast one has travelled is as old as the journey itself. With the arrival of the bicycle came previously unimagined opportunities for personal athletic achievement, the desire to record them ensuring that the cyclometer quickly became one of the most widely adopted accessories available to cycling's pioneers. Its modern equivalent is equally popular.

History

Early cycle odometers relied on a peg, usually attached to a spoke, to trip a peg wheel and thereby turn a clockwork mechanism. This recorded the number of revolutions it made and, from counting them, determined the distance covered. Odometers suitable for a range of specific wheel sizes were made. Any difference between measured and notional tyre circumference could be resolved by calculation to give an accurate figure for the rider's log. The eddy current-type speedometers of the day were less popular with enthusiast cyclists, perhaps because the drive arrangement, comprising a flexible cable driven by a small wheel held against the tyre sidewall, was both cumbersome and vulnerable.

Clockwork odometers were superseded in the 1980s by electronic cycle computers able to display a wide range of information ranging from current and average riding speeds to daily and total distance. The fundamental principle remains the same; count the number of wheel revolutions and multiply by tyre circumference to find distance travelled. By counting the number of wheel revolutions per second or other time interval the computer can also calculate riding speed.

Development

A magnet attached to a spoke takes the place of the old-style peg and triggers a pulse every wheel revolution in a sensor, often mounted on the fork blade. The same arrangement can be used to record pedalling speed, or cadence, by attaching a magnet to a crank and a sensor to an adjacent frame spar such as the chainstay. The computer can be configured using a wheel size figure obtained from a chart or by measuring tyre circumference directly. Cyclists wanting even greater accuracy can ride a known distance of, say, 10 miles and compare it with the distance recorded on the computer. If it is, say, 1.3% greater, then the configured tyre circumference is 1.013 x the correct figure and can be adjusted accordingly.

So small, light and easy to use are the latest standalone cycle computers that questions of aesthetics, ease of fitment and range of function are the biggest considerations when choosing a model. Wireless operation is a bonus as it eliminates the unsightly and vulnerable cable that must otherwise run from the front wheel sensor to the computer mounting pad. If used, the cable should be wound around suitable cables with as much care as tape around handlebars in order to minimise its visual impact.

Cycle computers from Shimano and Campagnolo work in concert with the manufacturers' dual-control gear shift levers (see pp. 114–115) to show cadence and gear selection in addition to the usual functions. Sensors inside the shift mechanism detect the position of the indexed cable pulley wheel and, from this, determine which sprocket or chainring is in use. Provided the tooth count of both is known, the computer can calculate the overall gear ratio and then, from road speed, how fast the cyclist must be pedalling. A 'virtual' cadence is shown even when freewheeling and can reach knee-wrecking speeds on fast descents.

Many times more expensive but offering greatly expanded capabilities, GPS-enabled computers have created an entirely new riding environment in which personal performance indicators can be accurately recorded in exhaustive detail and uploaded to a computer for later analysis or even to a sports activity-sharing website such as Garmin Connect or Strava. Depending on the user's technological immersion, features such as elevation, rate of climb or descent and current gradient may compete for attention with calorie consumption, heart rate measurement and even interval training instructions.

Perhaps these computers' most useful features are their mapping and navigation functions. GPS positioning, which uses signals from, typically, four satellites to allow a navigation device to work out its precise location, allows the owner of a GPS-enabled computer to dispense with the bulk, hassle and vulnerability to weather of paper maps. Equipped with a GPS-enabled cycle computer and full suite of accessories, today's road bike is the complete recreational tool.

▶ The information provided by a GPS-enabled computer is an integral part of many road cyclists' cycling activities.

Power Meters

Cycling is particularly appealing to sports scientists for the simple reason that the way the cycle transmission works makes it relatively easy to measure a rider's power output. This, in turn, simplifies the task of using power measurement to assess parameters such as maximal oxygen consumption – VO_2 max – and physiological response to training load. For the road cyclist, power is a more useful measure than heart rate, perceived exertion or riding speed as it is a more accurate indicator of work rate. It is also constant, unlike heart rate, which can vary widely with physical condition and freshness. Power meters also measure heart rate if required.

▼ SRM of Germany introduced the first truly effective on-bike power measuring system; it remains state of the art today.

Measuring power

Power is defined as the amount of work done divided by the time taken to do it and is measured in watts. One watt (1W) is equal to one joule – or the energy expended in lifting one newton through one metre – per second. One horsepower is the power needed to lift 550lbs through a vertical distance of 1ft in one second and is roughly equal to 746W. Power output is time dependent and doing a given amount of work in half the time requires twice the power.

Rate of lift is the most basic way to measure power and can be determined by using a rope wrapped around a shaft to do the lifting. This makes a rotational system in which power is determined as the product of torque – the force making the shaft rotate about its axis – and angular velocity, or the shaft's speed of rotation. There are several rotating components in the road bike drivetrain suitable for hooking up to a device able to measure torque and angular velocity, making cycling the ideal means for measuring human physiological potential.

History

Early attempts from the 1880s onwards to measure power during cycling employed stationary ergometers. A typical design might connect the pedals and cranks via a chain to a flywheel which used friction to pull on a weighted belt, dragging the belt further around its circumference the faster the flywheel turned; similar arrangements are still in use today. While a useful way to measure power output, this and other types of laboratory based equipment were of no use on the road and it was not until the advent of the German Schoberer Rad Messtechnik (SRM) system in 1986 that it was possible to measure accurately cyclists' power while they rode.

The patented SRM system measures power at the interface between the right-hand crank and chainring and takes the place of the crank spider. Following its introduction, devices have been developed to measure power at other suitable locations on the cycle, with each having its pros and cons. Unsurprisingly, given that it was first on the scene, the SRM Powermeter is placed at the prime location for the purpose as it is easy to measure both rotational speed and torque. There is no power loss to friction or frame flex and the system is widely regarded as the most accurate. Fixed securely to the cycle, it is time consuming to swap to another machine; on the other hand, parts such as wheels can be changed without affecting the Powermeter.

The rear wheel is a similarly suitable location for measuring power output. The amount won't be the same as at the crank, as some will have been lost to drivetrain friction and to flex in the frame and cranks, but instead of total power the CycleOps PowerTap hub is able to determine precisely how much is propelling the cycle along. The system is based on a hub in which strain gauges measure the deformation of a sleeve that transmits drive torque from the freehub body to the hub barrel.

Later versions have eliminated the physical connection between the sensor unit and handlebar-mounted computer and rely instead on wireless transmission of data via the ANT+ protocol. PowerTap is easy to swap from one machine to another and is considerably less expensive than the SRM system, but inevitably limits the user to one specific rear wheel, likely to be better suited to either racing or training, per unit.

As pioneers of on-bike power measurement, SRM and PowerTap were able to occupy the prime locations for power measurement. It can be done elsewhere on the cycle but at the cost of considerable extra complexity. Heart-rate monitor manufacturer Polar's Power Output Sensor W.I.N.D. measures the speed of travel of the chain via a jockey wheel and chain tension via a sensor on the chainstay and uses the two to derive power output. Working in partnership with the Polar CS600 cycle computer, it is light, easy to install and versatile but falls short of the +/- 2% accuracy claimed for the benchmark SRM system.

▼ PowerTap's power measuring device is found in the rear hub; the matching front ensures the wheels can be fitted as a pair.

Development

The iBike meter approaches the problem from the opposite direction, measuring the various forces opposing the cyclist such as wind resistance and gravity and, from them, calculating how much power must be produced to travel at the given speed.

The location that offers the most possibilities, however, is at the point where the foot applies force – the pedal. This is as close to the action as the power meter can get. More importantly, measurement at the pedals holds out the possibility of gathering information unavailable at the other end of the cranks. That's because the cranks are turned by force applied at a tangent to their circle of rotation; a meter located inboard of them only 'sees' tangential force. Since this is what generates torque, it does not affect the measurement of power output.

The advantage of measuring force at the pedal stems from the fact that no cyclist, however adept at pedalling, applies it purely at a tangent throughout the pedal circle. Some force is applied radially, or along the length of the crank. This does nothing to turn the pedals and may be counted as wasted effort – and it can be measured at the pedal using a suitable design.

The first to arrive on the market was the Polar LOOK KeO Power pedal system with Garmin's Vector pedals not far behind. Both employ strain gauges – eight in the case of the LOOK pedals – grouped around the axle to measure the way it flexes as force is applied. The axle of the LOOK pedal must be aligned with the cranks during installation so the system knows whether pedal force is being applied radially or tangentially – or, more likely, both at once. Crank length must also be dialled in to allow the computer to calculate torque. A reed switch in the pedal body measures cadence.

The data acquired by the various sensors and gauges is sent via Bluetooth Low Energy transmission to the accompanying Polar cycle computer, which then translates it into power output accurate, according to Polar, to +/– 2%. The pedals themselves only measure power and cadence and the computer needs a speed sensor and heart rate monitor to provide a comprehensive array of information, but since the system replaces a component – the pedals – that would be fitted in any case, it adds little to the weight of the cycle.

The layout of the strain gauges around the axle ensures that the Polar LOOK system can measure force applied to the pedals in any plane, meaning that it would be possible to separate tangential and radial pedalling forces and derive figures for total work done by the rider and, by comparing the two, for pedalling efficiency.

The same may be expected of the Garmin Vector pedals and of the long-awaited Brim Brothers system, which measures force applied at the interface between shoe sole and cleat. While the two pedal systems provide exceptional ease of exchange between cycles, the Brim Brothers design, which is entirely contained within the shoe and cleat assembly, will be even more versatile – when it arrives.

Power measurement during riding has revolutionised cycle training, providing coaches and sports scientists with vast quantities of highly relevant and valuable information. It has also given cyclists themselves something more to enjoy when riding; a true measure of exactly how hard they are working.

▶ Polar LOOK KeO
Power pedals

► The electrical contacts for Garmin's Vector power-measuring pedals are hidden inside the ends of the axles.

CALCULATING POWER

Cycling power is calculated by dividing work done by the time taken to do it. The time taken is done by measuring the rotational speed of a component in the same way that a cycle computer works out riding speed by counting how many times a wheel rotates per second. To calculate the amount of work done, strain gauges are attached to some component part that is strained – deformed – elastically when force is applied to the pedals. In a PowerTap hub, for example, this is a sleeve inside the barrel, which is twisted as it transmits pedalling force from the cassette to the hub barrel.

If loaded in tension, or pulled, the material will stretch; in compression, it will shorten. The strain gauges, which comprise a thin metallic foil in a grid pattern held in an insulating backing strip, are bonded to the surface of the part to be loaded and, as they stretch or compress with it, their electrical resistance changes. This resistance change, which can be measured with great accuracy, is used to determine the amount of deformation in the component; since it is known how much force is required to deform the part by any given amount, the force applied by the cyclist can be calculated. The meter then factors in the distance of the gauges from the centre of rotation, i.e. the lever arm length, to calculate torque.

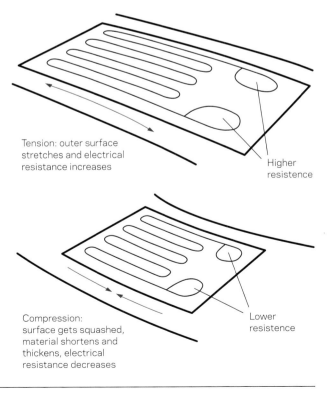

Tension: outer surface stretches and electrical resistance increases

Higher resistence

Compression: surface gets squashed, material shortens and thickens, electrical resistance decreases

Lower resistence

Mudguards

Competition cycles don't wear mudguards, or fenders as they are known in the US; they add weight, catch the air and generally slow cycling down. They also tend to spoil the appearance of the cycle unless it has clearly been designed to have them. On the other hand, they add greatly to the utility of the cycle and, for touring and long-distance riding in adverse conditions, are almost obligatory.

Form and function

Their function is self-evident; they are designed to keep water and muck thrown up by the tyres from reaching the rider and, to a lesser extent, the rest of the cycle. They are worth having not just when it is raining but at any time when the road surface is wet and they do more than simply keep the rider and rig clean and dry.

Water washed up from the road carries in suspension anything from fine particles of grit to rotten organic material and its accompanying microbial life; it is unpleasant stuff that can pose a health hazard via cuts and grazes or if ingested after it lands on the mouthpiece of a drinking bottle. Grit and, in winter, road salt greatly accelerate wear and corrosion of vulnerable parts and grit in particular rapidly degrades the fabric of cycling clothes. Effective mudguards minimise the impact of these problems.

Not all mudguards are equally effective. Ideally, guards should wrap as much of the wheel's circumference as is practical and should possess deep valances or sidewalls to trap water and prevent it from spraying sideways. They should be light but sturdy to prevent rubbing on tyres and rattle-free, to avoid making any noise that might inhibit enjoyment of the ride. And they should be durable, as in corrosion resistant, tough and hard to bend.

◄ Many attempts have been made to design road bike mudguards that are quickly installed and removed. Few match the performance of fixed mudguards.

Development

Early efforts to meet these demanding requirements were only partially successful. Mudguards made of leather proved apt to soften and soak up water, becoming increasingly heavy; those made of tin plate or thin pressed steel sheet were heavy from the start, rust-prone and easy to bend. Aluminium mudguards have long had their advocates and the traditional sort, especially when embossed with a hammered finish, look great aesthetically. They are also acceptably light, but tend to amplify noise and are easily damaged.

The advent of celluloid plastic mudguards heralded a new era of comfortable cycling; the classic Bluemel's label offered models in a variety of profiles and in bright colours with evocative names such as 'Club Special' and 'Lightweight'. They were light and didn't corrode, but the plastic material used was easily damaged and they were quickly superseded by the superior ESGE laminated aluminium and CAB plastic design when it arrived in the 1980s.

So good were the ESGE mudguards that, after some three decades in production largely unchanged, more recently under the SKS label, they remain the first choice for serious users. They feature a device called the Secu-Clip, which allows the stays on the front guard to become detached from the fork mounting in the event of an object becoming lodged between the tyre and guard. If this can't happen, the object may carry the end of the guard around as the wheel rotates, bunching it under the fork crown and locking the wheel with disastrous consequences.

They are not perfect; the aluminium strip incorporated into the middle of the plastic guard tends to corrode from any opening to the elements and the aluminium rivets used to attach the stainless steel stay brackets suffer from galvanic corrosion. They are sombre and utilitarian in appearance, work best on bikes with plenty of clearance between tyres and frame and are, inevitably, time consuming to remove when the sun comes out.

If maximum coverage is not the priority, there are plenty of other options. The most basic is the ungainly mountain bike-style clip-on paddle that clips behind the saddle and does nothing more than protect the rider's seat. One such design, the San Marco Ass-Saver, makes this limitation abundantly clear. More effective are models such as SKS Race Blades, which can be fitted to cycles lacking clearance for full length guards. Designed to be quick to fit and remove, they are easily displaced by a knock and difficult to install with precision. Gaps on either side of the brake calipers reduce the effectiveness of these otherwise useful items.

Better in this respect is the innovative Crud Road Racer, which approaches mudguard design from a novel perspective. Where traditional 'guards are made to be as rigid as possible to keep them from flexing and rubbing the tyres, the Road Racer is flexible and fragile looking. To keep it from rubbing on the tyre, it relies on fibrous brushes, which rub against the wheel rim brake tracks, to keep the precision-moulded 'guard centred over the tyre. This 'floating' action is remarkably effective and allows Crud to dispense with the weighty hardware required to keep a conventional 'guard in place. Weighing just 180g per pair, Crud Road Racers are even suitable for close-clearance competition cycles.

▶ Full-length mudguards are as important a fitment to a touring bike as a sturdy rear pannier rack.

Luggage

While light and apparently delicate, the road bike is capable of carrying a useful load provided it is fitted with suitable luggage. Many cyclists decline to do so and prefer to ride with a rucksack but, unless travelling a short distance or with a very light load, would be better advised to let the cycle do the work.

◀ The under-saddle pouch or pack barely counts as luggage but serves a valuable purpose whatever it is asked to contain.

Carrying light loads

Weight carried on the rider's back bears down through the pelvis on the saddle, applying additional pressure to an often sorely tested area. It is carried high, reducing stability, and prevents sweat from evaporating. Perhaps the only clear disadvantage of carrying luggage on the cycle instead is weight; a laden road bike feels relatively sluggish and unresponsive. Side panniers also add to wind resistance, but luggage carefully chosen and properly fitted only adds to the capabilities of the machine.

Given the layout of the road bike, there is limited space available for carrying stuff. The one to be avoided unless absolutely necessary is the area within the frame's main triangle. Although hanging a bag from the underside of the top tube may seem an attractive option, it will have to be narrow if it is not to foul the rider's knees. It will also affect the bike's handling in side winds and, unless small, may compete for space with bottle cages.

Small, light loads may be carried in a bag slung from the handlebars. This is the position traditionally favoured by French randonneurs and fast tourists. Convenient for the retrieval of a camera or money and, control cables permitting, the bag fills an inviting space. It may hang directly from the bars, taking up hand room, or from a supporting bracket, adding to the weight over the front wheel. Overloading a handlebar bag may affect the bike's steering and stability.

Ideally slung from loops provided for the purpose as part of the saddle structure, the traditional British saddlebag would appear to occupy the ideal position, behind the rider and out of the wind. However, unless supported from the underside, it offers limited load capacity and has a disconcerting tendency to sway when riding out of the saddle. It can also be time consuming to remove from the cycle. Against this must be put the saddlebag's undeniable visual appeal and its convenient height when rummaging for mislaid items.

The modern take on this traditional piece of luggage sits on a boom clamped to and cantilevered from the seat post. Needing no further means of attachment to the cycle, the seatpost pack is quick and easy to fit to any bike while the, usually, long and narrow bag shape keeps wind resistance to a minimum. A heavily loaded pack will, however, put great stress on the seatpost unless the boom is supported by struts from the seatstays, leaving the layout best suited to the fast tourist riding light.

Carrying heavy loads

When it comes to carrying a substantial load or carrying any luggage with maximum security, one or two panniers attached to a rack and sited either side of a wheel will prove the best option. Panniers can, of course, be fitted at both the front and rear of the cycle but such an arrangement only adds to the temptation to carry too much. The rule that luggage expands to fill the space available applies with

particular effect to nominal rear panniers, which are cavernous in comparison to any other type of cycle luggage. A useful exercise in keeping weight down is to try to fit everything into smaller front panniers and then put them at the rear of the bike.

Panniers are often fitted with external straps, pouches and clips of dubious value. Not only do loose straps pose something of a hazard, but they catch the wind. Similarly, pouches designed to hold drinking bottles add significantly to the external profile of the pannier if used as intended. Performance-minded tourists will opt instead for panniers with a minimum of external clutter.

Racks and their associated panniers are best mounted on cycles provided with suitable threaded bosses, mainly because the weight of a rack and two well-stuffed panniers can overwhelm the C-clips usually used as an alternative means of attachment. Pannier racks themselves must be as rigid as possible to prevent luggage sway, which will affect handling.

The finest racks are constructed of small-diameter thin-wall steel tubing and can weigh well under half a kilogramme, but racks made using solid aluminium rod offer comparable performance at a lower price. They are, however, more susceptible to fatigue failure and harder to repair should it happen. When it comes to loaded cycling, steel is the real deal.

▶ Pannier bags mounted either side of a rack generally prove the most effective way to carry moderate amounts of luggage.

Tools

Although not strictly a component part of the bike, portable tools are nevertheless a vital accessory carried by most cyclists except when racing. Tools are heavy and carrying them unwelcome, so choosing exactly which tools to carry is a very personal decision that depends as much on the rider's ability to use them as on the likelihood of encountering a problem. Many cyclists believe the most and, indeed, only useful tool in an emergency to be a mobile telephone.

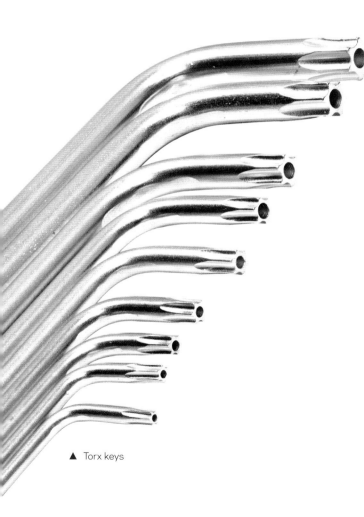

▲ Torx keys

Repair essentials

Most mechanical problems are, however, minor and easily resolved by a competent rider using tools that will fit inside a small saddle pack. Of course, some mechanical failures are beyond the scope of roadside repair, which is where either the mobile phone or the funds for a train fare come in handy.

Fortunately, cycles today are fundamentally more reliable than those of even a couple of decades ago and the serious failures commonly experienced by cyclists of yesteryear are all but unknown. Tales of wrapping fatigue-fractured frame tubes in wire and soldering them over an open fire, or of clamping a small vice to a handlebar in order to hold a cotter pin while filing it to fit, surely sound far-fetched to modern ears and the means to carry them out are unlikely to be part of any current cyclist's toolkit.

Multi-tool
Nevertheless, there is a place in touring and audax riding for the generalist multi-tool, which usually boasts pliers and a small knife blade. With one, resourceful cyclists have been known to fix a broken chain using wire cut from a fence or to fashion items such as wooden plugs to join broken tubes.

Spanner
The most common mechanical problem to afflict cycling is surely the puncture (see pp. 182–183). In any case, puncture repair is best carried out with the wheel removed, which is easy enough on a cycle with quick-release wheels. Fixed-wheel machines, which retain a devoted following amongst British road cyclists, almost always use track nuts

▲ Chain tool in use

▲ Spoke key

to secure the rear wheel and these require a suitable spanner. The stylist's choice is not an adjustable wrench but a ring spanner, usually 15mm across flats, of the type used by track cyclists; the design ensures a secure grip of the nut when applying the considerable torque required to tighten the wheel nuts.

Hex, Torx and spoke keys

Roadside adjustment, accident repair or non-routine maintenance of the modern cycle will almost certainly need a hex or Allen key. Hex keys, made of hardened steel, turn a screw with an internal hexagon drive or 'socket' head and for high-end cycles have entirely replaced the heavier and more bulky spanners required to turn an external hexagon head. A selection of hex keys in the sizes commonly used on cycles forms the basis of all cycle multi-tools.

A basic example may incorporate hex keys in the four most commonly used sizes: 3, 4, 5 and 6mm, along with flat-blade and Phillips-head screwdrivers, which are widely used on derailleur throw adjustment screws. Such a selection will, on most road bikes, allow the rider to carry out any small adjustments that may be required to items such as saddle height, handlebar alignment and derailleur gear operation.

As this is insufficient for all but the most minor of adjustments, cyclists prepared to tackle more challenging maintenance tasks will carry a tool with a much wider array of bits including items such as a short, fat 8mm hex key, which can be used on some models to tighten a loose crank bolt, and Torx keys, which possess a six-sided lobular tip

that can transmit a higher torque than the same size hex key. Torx heads are increasing used for high-torque but space-limited applications such as chainring bolts.

While a spoke key suitable for the wheels fitted to the cycle will prove invaluable should a spoke break or the rim get dented by a hole, the one repairable component that will leave a cyclist stranded should it fail is the chain, which makes a chain breaker – best used in conjunction with a joining link (see pp. 104–105) – arguably the most important item in the kit. The force required to press a chain pin through its side plates is substantial and the construction of a reliable chain breaker equally so. To save weight and space, the chain tool may be incorporated in the multi-tool.

Tool pouch

The most convenient way to carry a collection of tools is in a pouch or pack tucked away behind the saddle. Packs situated behind the handlebar stem have no place on a road bike. Saddle packs are available in a wide range of sizes; some feature zipper-secured extensible sections that open up to accommodate extra material as required.

Most ingenuity, however, has been expended in devising ways to attach the pack to the saddle. Velcro® or hook-and-loop straps are popular and effective but lack the technical sophistication and appeal of the quick-release clips and clamps found on some models. Velcro® is, however, very light and packs thus secured have the further advantage of sitting very close to the saddle, rather than wobbling on a strut like some kind of exotic fruit waiting to be picked. As ever in cycling, light and simple is best.

Inflation

The first and most useful repair skill any cyclist learns is
fixing a puncture and not simply because, without those two
precious pockets of compressed gas, a bicycle is next to useless.
Punctures are, despite the advances in tyre technology seen over
the past decade, common enough to make starting a journey
without the means to repair one something of a rash act.

Puncture repair

Repairing a puncture is, for the clincher tyre user, generally
a simple task taking a few minutes and made quicker by
fitting a spare inner tube instead of attempting to repair the
punctured example. Well-prepared cyclists carry two spares
known to be airtight, wrap them in fabric for protection
against chafing caused by jiggling around in a saddle pack
and check them occasionally to make sure they still hold air.

It is, of course, unwise to expect to complete a ride with no
more than two punctures, so a repair kit may be carried as
back-up for the two spare tubes. Its contents will say much
about the outlook of the owner, who may be happy to carry
nothing more than a couple of 'instant' patches. These
items are coated with a type of glue supposed to provide
instant adhesion to a clean inner tube and, when they do
so, undoubtedly make a quick repair, if not one that can be
relied on to last for more than a few months.

Occasionally the glue fails to work as expected, which is
when the traditional repair method wins outright. The kits
supplied by TipTop of Germany are typical of the latest
type and invariably provide a reliable, long-lasting repair if
used according to the instructions. While most of these are
not onerous, one in particular is often ignored. Inevitably, it
is the one that may not be ignored and failure of the patch
to adhere invariably results. The solvent in the glue, or
rubber solution, must be allowed to evaporate entirely
before the patch is applied. This can take a seemingly
endless five minutes, but any solvent remaining will prevent
the solution applied to the tube from making a chemical
bond with the adhesive layer on the back of the patch.

If done correctly, the bond between patch and tube will be
as strong as the rubber itself and there is no practical reason,
provided each hole is small enough be patched, why a tube
should not be repaired as many times as the owner wishes.
An informal limit of six patches is widely respected by
those who go to the trouble of repairing their tubes.

► Inner tube repair patches and a tube of rubber solution form the bedrock of the competent cyclist's roadside repair kit.

Repair kit

The repair kit may contain an assortment of potentially useful items such as a valve extender tube, a small plastic key to fit the removal part of a Presta valve, a sharp craft knife blade that can be used to scrape clean the surface of an inner tube and a piece of old tubular tyre. This is to be used as a tyre 'boot', covering from the inside of the tyre any cut in the carcass through which the inner tube might bulge and burst. Some parts manufacturers offer ready-made tyre boots, but the satisfaction to be had from using one cut from an old tyre is immense. Tubular tyre carcass is best for the purpose because it is thin and supple but strong enough to retain the tube. A tyre that has been booted remains potentially dangerous and should be replaced as soon as possible.

Tyre levers are supplied in bundles of three in order that one may be lost without causing difficulties. Two levers may be needed to remove a tight clincher tyre but one is usually enough if using correct technique and many experienced cyclists, who nevertheless will always carry at least one, can remove even a stubborn tyre using just fingers and thumbs. The temptation, when trying to refit a tight tyre, to resort to levers should be resisted as they are apt to pinch the inner tube.

Cyclists who favour tubular tyres, also known as 'tubs' or 'sew-ups', rarely attempt a repair at the roadside but simply fit a replacement or look for a lift, since repair is a long-winded process. The experienced tubular tyre rider will carry a used spare, which will have some glue left stuck to its base tape from previous fitment. This will ensure the tyre stays put, although it is unwise to put too much faith in a freshly fitted spare when cornering.

In case of a second puncture, the hardened tub enthusiast will carry a repair kit and won't be afraid to use it. This means removing the tub's base tape and cutting the stitching adjacent to the puncture before locating and repairing the hole in the tube. The next stage provides the challenge; the carcass must be sewn back up using the sturdy linen thread and needle supplied in the repair kit and a suitable stitching technique. Finally, the base tape must be glued back in place, which in turn means carrying a tube of tub cement.

Pumping

Repairing inner tubes and tyres is only one side of the business of riding on pneumatic tyres. Once repaired, they must also be inflated using one of the many more or less effective portable methods devised for the purpose.

Mini-pump

Of these, easily the least effective is the mini-pump. The name gives the game away; such pumps are small or, rather, short. Cycle pumps generally operate on the plunger principle; a piston on a rod is pushed through a tube connected to the tyre valve, reducing the volume of the space inside and increasing the pressure of the trapped air pro rata. Road bike tyres hold air at a pressure of around 100psi or 7bar (atmospheres). To reach this pressure, the piston in a conventional pump must reduce the total air volume at the start of the stroke to one seventh at its end.

The total air volume includes the 'dead' volume between the piston at the end of its stroke and the seating face of the valve. This dead volume is at a practical minimum in a pump with integral chuck that clamps directly to the valve stem and is greater in proportion to the stroke, the shorter the pump. Add to this the small volume of air compressed by each stroke and it is obvious why owners of mini-pumps struggle to inflate their tyres to the desired pressure. If it is to be carried on the bike, a mini-pump also requires an ugly bracket that usually sits under a bottle cage; most road cyclists prefer to stick the pump in a jersey pocket.

▲ The workshop or stirrup pump can't be carried on a ride but should be used regularly to ensure tyres are kept at optimum operating pressure.

▼ Mini-pumps are better than they were and look sleek but remain the choice of the optimistic.

Full-length pump

Superior in most respects, including ease of inflation, is the full-length frame-fitting pump, which employs a spring-loaded plunger handle that permits the pump to fit snugly and securely between frame tubes. As the handle will only accommodate a small size variation, these pumps are offered in several lengths. The most popular but visually least attractive location for a frame-fitting pump is the underside of the top tube. Some touring cyclists prefer to place the pump beside a seatstay to keep it out of the way should the cycle need to be carried. This arrangement generally requires the provision of a locating peg and to some extent nullifies the supposed advantage of fitment direct to the frame.

Chuck

Hand pumps of all sizes usually feature an integral chuck, which can be quickly pressed over the valve to speed inflation. Using these chucks can be tricky, however, and it is easy to bend the slender thread of a Presta valve toggle nut. This has led to the reintroduction of the pump tube, which provides a flexible, easy-to-use connection that must be screwed onto the valve thread. The additional dead volume is, for many, a small price to pay for ease of use.

Gas canister

The fastest way to inflate a tyre – and the easiest to carry – is to use a gas canister. A standard 16g canister delivers in seconds a charge of carbon dioxide sufficient to inflate a 700c tyre to riding pressure. An adaptor is needed; of the many types, the best are those that incorporate a trigger that releases gas as required, since this makes it possible to partially inflate the inner tube for ease of installation. In any case, using CO_2 to inflate a tyre is a short-term measure as the gas leaks through the inner tube walls over a few days. To get around the fact that each canister will only inflate one tyre, manufacturers have come up with the combined hand pump and gas canister adaptor. The disadvantages are self-evident.

▼ Even the humble water bottle or bidon can look smart when held in a carbon-fibre cage.

Deconstructed Parts of a Bike

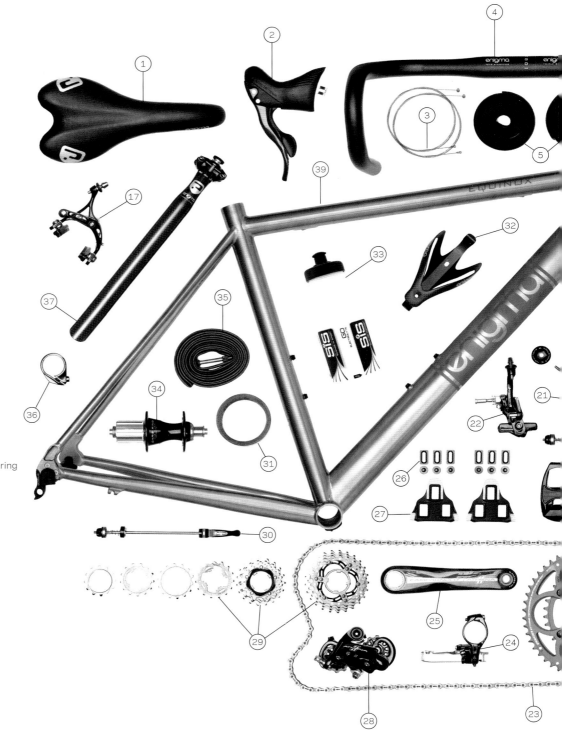

1. Saddle
2. Shifter
3. Cable inners
4. Handlebar
5. Bar tape
6. Bar-end plugs
7. Shifter
8. Rim
9. Spokes
10. Stem
11. Stem bolts
12. Tyre
13. Bottom assembly bearing
14. Fork
15. Rim tape
16. Inner tube
17. Chainset
18. Pedals
19. Quick-release skewer
20. Top assembly bearing
21. Front hub
22. Front caliper
23. Chain
24. Front derailleur
25. Crank
26. Cleat bolts
27. Cleats
28. Rear derailleur
29. Cassette
30. Quick release skewer
31. Rim tape
32. Bottle cage
33. Bottle
34. Rear hub
35. Inner tube
36. Seat post clamp
37. Seat post
38. Rear caliper
39. Frame headset

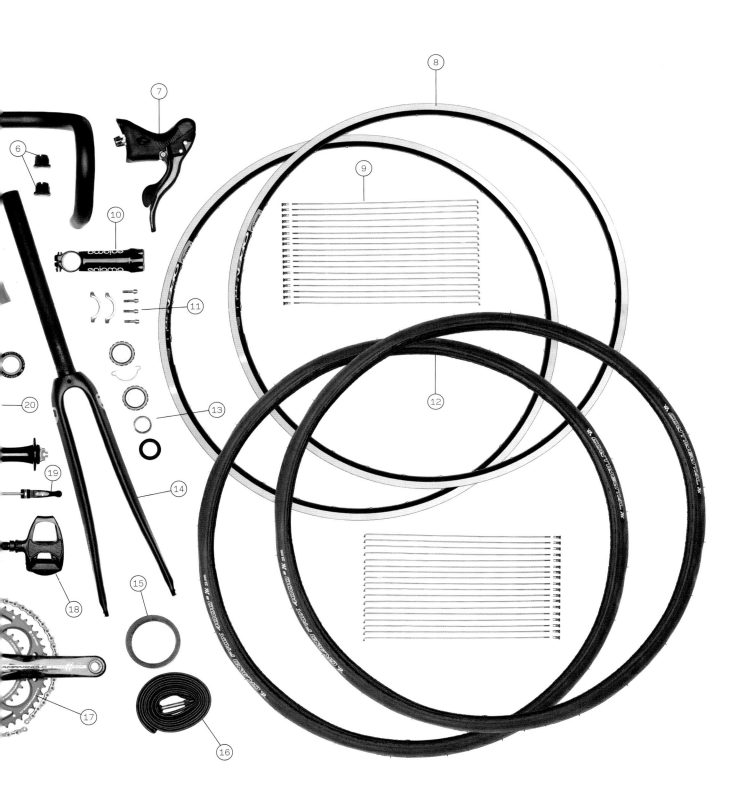

Glossary

Alloy: A mixture of at least two elements, at least one of which is a metal, which in solid form offers different and usually more desirable mechanical characteristics than the pure base elements

Annular precession: The tendency for a component to turn in the opposite direction to a coaxially rotating part. It can be imagined by rotating a pencil around the inside of the looped index finger and thumb; the pencil will rotate backwards as it travels forwards around the loop

Axial: Extending parallel to the axis of some cylindrical or rotating component

BCD: Or bolt circle diameter; the diameter of the virtual circle on which several bolts securing the chainrings to the crank spider are located

Bearing: A component that supports and locates a moving part, constrains its plane of motion and, usually, minimises friction between it and the non-moving part of the machine

Brazing: The joining of parent metals using a metal filler rod of lower melting temperature and relying on the filler's penetration of the joint by capillary action

Butting: The process of providing extra material at the points of greatest stress; the walls of a butted tube are thicker at the ends, where the bending stresses during riding are greatest and where the tubes are heated during the building process, than in the middle

Chainset: Crankset with chainring or rings attached

Cleat: Steel or plastic part, affixed to the sole of a cycling shoe, that engages with jaws on the pedal to provide a secure attachment when pedalling

CNC-machining: Computer numerical control; the travel of machine tool cutting heads is controlled by computer to ensure a consistently high level of accuracy

Compact: Of frame; typified by a top tube sloping down to a seat tube shortened in comparison to that of a traditional frame. Of gearing; a chainset equipped with smaller than standard chainrings e.g. 50/34 instead of 53/39

Crankset: Assembly comprising left- and right-hand crank arms and bottom bracket axle

Derailleur: System of variable gearing that works by derailing the drive chain from one sprocket or chainring to another that is smaller or larger, thus changing gear ratio

Diamond frame: Cycle frame notable for a diamond or lozenge form comprising front and rear triangles joined at a central seat tube

Dropout: Locating tang for the front or rear wheel spindle equipped with open-ended slot that allows the spindle to drop free when the securing mechanism is released

Extrusion: Forming process in which the extruded material is forced through a shaped die to produce a bar of precise dimensions and with a potentially complex cross-section

Fixed gear: Transmission offering only one gear ratio, aka single-speed

Fixed-wheel: Transmission lacking a freewheel mechanism so the pedals rotate at a speed fixed to that of the driving wheel

Flange: Disc-shaped radial projection from the barrel of a hub

Forging: The shaping of metal using applied compressive force

Freehub: Rear hub for derailleur gearing equipped with integral freewheeling body on which are mounted several sprockets

Gauge: Thickness, typically of a wire spoke or tube wall

Gear: Distance travelled per pedal revolution; UK practice is to express the gear ratio as the effective diameter, not circumference, of the driving wheel

Groupset: Coherent collection of components found on the bicycle; usually includes chainset, brake calipers, derailleur mechanisms and brake/dual-control levers. Usually grouped under a common name e.g. Shimano Dura-Ace, Campagnolo Record. May include wheel hubs

Hollowtech II: Influential Shimano crankset design notable for external bottom bracket bearings and axle incorporated in the right-hand crank

Hub gear: Variable gearing system with, usually, one or more epicyclic gear trains contained within and protected by the rear hub shell

Hydraulic: System of force transfer relying on flexible hose and the incompressibility of a 'hydraulic' fluid, usually either mineral oil or ether-based glycol

Indexing: The provision of specific positions for a gear control lever that correspond with the chosen gear ratio

Integrated: Incorporated within major component rather than fitted as self-contained unit e.g. headset

ISIS Drive: 'Open' bottom bracket axle and crank interface standard featuring 10 splines at each end of the axle

J-bend: Wire wheel spoke with a J-shaped bend at the non-threaded end that fits in a hole in the hub flange. A mushroom head prevents the spoke pulling through the hole

Jockey wheel: Chain guide wheel found as one of a pair in the rear derailleur mechanism

Juy, Lucien: Founder of the French component manufacturer Simplex

Knuckle: One of two substantial parts at each end of the deformable parallelogram of a rear derailleur mechanism

Lubrication: Means of reducing friction, heat and wear between moving parts. Often the subject of heated debate amongst cyclists

Lugs: Reinforcing sockets housing frame tubes at their conjunctions

Mektronic: Seminal electronic derailleur gear shifting system introduced by Mavic

Monobloc: Carbon-fibre or other composite part moulded in one piece rather than as several parts later bonded together

Newton: International System of Units derived unit of force; at the surface of the Earth, approximates to 102g

Nipple: Pear-shaped nut threaded over the end of a wire wheel spoke to permit application of tension

Nokon: Alternative to Bowden wire outer casing comprising articulating segments, each with a ball or socket at each end

Oversized: A component larger in some respect, usually diameter, than the historic 'standard' size

Pneumatic: Relying on compressed air or other gas to provide some mechanical effect. In cycling, pneumatic tyres provide extremely effective lightweight suspension

Profile: Shape or cross section; may be 'low', as in some cycle parts designed to be aerodynamically effective

Quick release: Mechanism that permits rapid wheel removal; in brake calipers, is a means of widening the gap between brake block to permit the passage of the inflated tyre

Quill: Traditional pedal designed for use with toe clips and notable for upturned projection on outer end of cage or traditional handlebar stem with downward-projecting 'quill' tube that telescopes into the fork steerer tube

Radial: Extending directly outwards from a centre as the radius of a circle

Rake, fork: The distance by which the front wheel spindle's centre line is offset from the steering bearing's centre line. Usually seen as curvature of the fork blade

Rigidity: The mechanical property of resistance to deflection under load

Safety bicycle: Improvement over the ordinary, high-wheeler or penny-farthing bicycle and identified by chain drive to the rear wheel

Seat angle: Angle of the seat tube with the horizontal. Tends to be around 73° for upright cycling

Shell, bottom bracket: Part of the cycle frame housing the bottom bracket bearings

Spline: Ridge or projection extending axially beyond the surface of a cylinder or barrel and designed to permit the transmission of torque

Sportive: Supposedly non-competitive organised mass-participation cycle ride, usually run over challenging terrain

Sprocket: Toothed chain wheel fitted to the rear wheel

Stays: Struts that make up the rear triangle of the diamond frame

Glossary (continued)

Teflon: Slippery solid used as friction-reducing layer or additive

TIG: Tungsten inert gas welding process; an inert gas, usually argon, shields the weld pool from contamination by oxygen while the welding arc is struck between the work and a non-consumable tungsten electrode, melting the edges of the work pieces to create a weld pool. Filler rod of the same metal is added to the pool if needed

Torsion: Twisting force

Tubeset: Collection of eight tubes that make up the traditional diamond frame. May include the tubes that make up the front fork

UCI: Union Cycliste Internationale; the world governing body for cycle competition

Ultegra: Second-tier Shimano road groupset

V-Brake: Shimano trademark for linear-pull rim brakes

Wedge nut: Applies radial force at the tip of a quill handlebar stem to jam it against the inside of the fork steerer

Welding: Joining metal by melting the work piece to create a weld pool. Filler of the same metal is added to the pool if needed

Westwood: Archaic rim pattern suitable for use with roller-lever rod brakes and still popular on utility bicycles in developing countries

XTR: Top-level Shimano mountain bike groupset; has influenced Shimano road groupset design

Young's modulus: Ratio of applied stress to strain, or deflection; a measure of a material's stiffness

Zicral: Trade name for 7075 aluminium alloy

Further Reading

Berto, Frank; *The Dancing Chain: History and Development of the Derailleur Bike* (Van Der Plas: 2008)

Burke, Edmund R; *High-Tech Cycling* (Human Kinetics: 2003)

Facchinetti & Rubino; *Campagnolo: 75 Years of Cycling Passion* (Velo Press: 2008)

Fotheringham, William; *Cyclopedia: It's All About the Bike* (Yellow Jersey Press: 2010)

Heine, Jan; *The Golden Age of Handbuilt Bicycles: Craftsmanship, Elegance and Function* (Rizzoli International Publications: 2009)

Joseph, Lionel; *The First Century of the Bicycle and Its Accessories* (Private: 1996)

Moore, Richard; *Bike!* (Aurum Press: 2012)

Ritchie, Andrew; *King of the Road: An Illustrated History of Cycling* (Wildwood House: 1975)

Index

A

accessories 167–183
Accles and Pollock 20
adjusting barrels 12
AeroLink 128
ALAN 24, 42
Allsop Softride 48
aluminium 16, 17, 24–25
Ambrosia 149
American Classic 74
anatomy overview 12–13
Arai 144
Araya 61
Ariel, The 53
Armstrong, Lance 22
Asso 61
Atax 149
AVA 149, 153
Ax-Lighteness 150

B

Bartali, Gino 109
Bartlett, William 64
BCD (Bolt Circle Diameter) 96
Berner-Bikes 111
Beyl, Jean 88
Bianchi 36
Billato 18
Binda 87
Binda, Alfredo 87
blades 43
Bluemel 175
Boardman, Chris 116
bolt circle diameter (BCD) 96
boneshaker bicycles 53
Bontrager 61, 128
Booty, Ray 120
bottom bracket assemblies 32, 41, 98–103
Bowden 108, 127, 130, 138, 143
Bowden, Ernest 127
brake cables 12, 34, 130–131
brake casings 131
brake hoods 12
brake mounts 45
brake pads 12
brakes 12, 125–145
Brooks 151, 157, 161
Burgess, Gerry 134
butting 36
Byrne, Richard 88

C

CAB 175
cables 12, 34, 130–131
Calfee, Craig 18
caliper brakes 128
Cambio Campagnolo 109
Campagnolo
  brake systems 128, 129, 134, 135
  cassettes 112
  chainsets 96
  clipless pedals 88
  cycle computers 169
  Electronic Power Shift (EPS) 117
  Ergopower 114, 115
  Gran Sport 110, 162, 163
  hubs 74, 76
  Record 77, 110, 128, 163
  Shamal 58, 61
  Super Record 87, 110, 111, 164
  Tipo Paris–Roubaix 109
  Ultra-Shift 113
Campagnolo, Tullio 43, 78
Cancellara, Fabian 48
Cannondale 36, 41, 49, 94, 102
Canyon 165
carbon-fibre 16, 17, 18–19
cassettes 12, 112–113
centre-pull brakes 138, 139
Cervélo 39, 102
CFD (Computational Fluid Dynamics) 55, 61
chainstays 12, 32, 39
chain tools 179
chainrings 12, 96–97
chains 12, 104–105
chainsets 90–97
Chris King 77
Christophe 87
Christophe, Eugène 38, 87
Cinelli
  handlebars 149, 151, 153, 154
  pedals 86, 88
  saddles 157
clincher tyres 64, 67
clipless pedal systems 84–89
CODA 94
Colnago 18, 43
Colnago, Ernesto 43
Columbus Spirit 20
Computational Fluid Dynamics (CFD) 55, 61
computers 168–173
contact points 147–165

corrosion inhibitors 165
cotter pin cranks 91
Coventry Chain Co. 105
crank arms 12, 91–95
cranksets 12
cross frames 29, 30
crowns 43
Crud Road Racer 175
cycle computers 168–173
CycleOps PowerTap 171
cycling shoes 84–85
Cyclo company 110

D

Deda 150
derailleur gear systems 105, 106–111, 114
Desgrange, Henri 107, 119
Detto Pietro 84
DiaCompe 129
diamond frames 27, 28, 29, 30–31
differentiated braking 135
disc brakes 125, 142–143
down tubes 12, 32, 35
drivetrains 83–123
dropouts 32, 38, 43
dropped handlebars 148–151
drum brakes 144–145
DT Swiss 71
dual-control gear shift levers 169
dual-pivot brake calipers 134
Duclos-Lassalle, Gilbert 49
Duegi 84
Dunlop, John Boyd 62
Dunlop Pneumatic Tyre Co. 64

E

Eadie 119
Edco 112
Egg, Oscar 108
electronic shifting 116–117
Endrick 60, 128
Enigma 20–21, 22–23, 150, 152, 155
ESGE 175
EVA foam 150, 151

F

fenders 174–175
Fiber Grip 165
fixed-wheel transmissions 122–123
Fizik 151, 158, 160
Flema 22
fork blades 12

fork crowns 12
fork rake 44
framesets 16, 18, 20, 24, 27–49
freehubs 80–81
freewheel mechanisms 80, 81, 112, 113
front derailleurs 12
front dropouts 12
front forks 42–45, 43
front-wheel driven designs 29

G
Garmin 169, 173
GB 134, 149
gear cable stops 35
Giant 31, 37, 44
Gitane 33
Godefroot, Walter 49
GPS-enabled computers 169
Grout, W. H. J. 53, 72, 73

H
handlebar stems 152–155
handlebar tape 150
handlebars 12, 148–151
head tubes 32, 33
headsets 46–47
HED 61
Hed, Steve 61
Herse, Rene 153
Hex keys 179
Hinault, Bernard 33, 88
hub gears 118–121, 123
hubs 12, 74–77, 81
Huret 110
hydraulic brake systems 136–137

I
iBike meter 172
indexed gears 114
Indurain, Miguel 68, 88, 158
IscaSelle 158
IsoSpeed 48
ITM (Italmanubri) 149, 153, 154

J
Jeay roller cam brakes 128
joining/joints 40
Juy, Lucien 108

K
Kamm Virtual Foil (KVF) 33
Kelly, Sean 24, 88
Klein, Gary 24

L
La Vie Claire 18
leather saddles 157
LeMond, Greg 22, 88
levers 12
Lindley and Biggs 29, 48
linear-pull brakes 140–141
Litespeed 22
Lizard Skin 151
lock rings 123
Longhi, Mario 55
LOOK
    695 Aerolight 95, 140, 141
    forks 43
    linear-pull brakes 141
    pedal systems 85, 88, 89, 172
luggage 176–177, 179
Lyotard 87

M
Mafac 129, 138–139
Magne, Antonin 55
Magura 136
Maillard 112
Major Taylor 153
Mapei 1-2-3 18
materials 16–25
Mavic
    electronic shifting systems 116–117
    wheelsets 55, 58, 60, 61, 65, 71, 73
Merlin Metalworks 22
Michaux 53
Michelin 55, 63, 65
Microshift 114
Modolo 114, 128, 129
monocoque construction 18
mudguards 174–175
multi-tools 178
Museeuw, Johan 49

N
Nicol, Scot 22
nipples 72–73
Noah 141
NuVinci 121

O
O-Symetric 96
Ocaña, Luis 22
odometers 169
offsets 43
Olano, Abraham 68
Osgear 108

P
Palmer, J. F. 64
panniers 176, 177
Paul 139
pedals 12, 84–89
Pedersen, Mikael 31
penny-farthing bicycles 53
Petit-Breton, Lucien 119
Peugeot 18
Phantom, The 53
Philippe 149
Philips 22
Pinarello Paris 24
pinch flats 69
platform pedals 87
PMP 165
pneumatic tyres 48, 62–-65
Polar 171, 172
power meters/measurement 170–173
Power Tap 170
Pro 150
Profile 150
pumps 182–183
punctures 63, 68, 69, 180–181, 182

Q
quick-release wheel mechanisms 78–79
quill pedals 87
quill stems 152, 153, 154

R
rakes 43
rat-trap pedals 87
rear brake cables 34
rear derailleurs 12
rear dropouts 12
rear wheels 59
repair kits 178–179, 181
Resilion 128, 138
Resin Transfer Molding (RTM) 18
Reynold, Hans 105
Reynolds 20, 71
Reynolds, Alfred 20
Ridley 141
rim brakes 125
rims 12
road bikes, definition 11
RockShox 49
Rohloff 199, 120
Rolf Prima 74
roller chains 104–105
Rominger, Tony 18, 116
Rotor 94, 96, 155
Rover Safety Bike 30
Rudge Bicyclette 29, 30

S

Sablière, André 24
Sachs 114, 120
saddlebags 176–177, 179
saddles 12, 147, 156–161
San Marco 158, 175
Sapim 71
Schoberer Rad Messtechnik (SRM) 171
Scott 103
seat rails 12
seat tubes 32, 36–37
seatposts 12, 162–163
seatstays 12, 32, 39
Sedisport 105
Selle Italia 158, 159
semi-monocoque construction 18
shift controls 114–117
Shimano
    bottom bracket assemblies 103
    brake systems 129, 131, 134
    cassettes 112, 113
    cycle computers 169
    disc brake systems 143
    drum brake systems 144, 145
    dual-control gear shift levers 114
    Dura-Ace 81, 94, 114, 117, 128
    Freehub 80, 112
    Hollowtech II 95
    hub gears 120
    hubs 76
    hydraulic brake systems 136, 137
    linear-pull brakes 141
    pedal systems 86, 88, 89
    rear mechanism designs 111
    seatposts 164
    Shimano Total Integration (STI) 115
    wheelsets 73
shoe cleats 84–85
side-pull brakes 132–135, 133, 139
Simplex 108, 110, 114
Simpson, Tom 157
single-pivot side-pull brake calipers 133
single-speed bikes 123
skewer rods 79
SKS 175
spanners 178–179
Specialized 49
Speedplay 85, 88, 89
Speedwell Gear Case Co. 22
Spinergy 71
spoke keys 179
spoke nipples 72–73
spokes 12, 53, 58–59, 70–71
SR 153

SRAM
    brake systems 134, 136
    Double Tap dual control gear levers 114, 115
    hubs 120
    OpenGlide 113
    RED group 111, 113, 128
    WiFLi transmissions 96
SRM 171
Starley, James 30, 53
steel 16, 17, 20–21
steerer tubes 43, 44
stems 152–155
stiffness of frames 16–17, 24
Strava 169
Sturmey-Archer 114, 119, 120, 121, 123, 144
Sun Tour 114
Super Champion 108, 109
suspension 48–49

T

TA 87, 96
Tchmil, Andrei 49
Technique du Verre Tissé (TVT) 18, 40
Tecno Tube Torino (3T) 149, 153, 154
Teledyne Titan 22
Terront, Charles 63
Thomson, Robert William 62
threaded/threadless headsets 47
threadless handlebar stems 152, 154–155
3T 150
Thys, Philippe 119
TIG (Tungsten inert gas) welding 17, 24, 40, 153, 186
TIME Sport International 18, 85, 88, 89, 155
TipTop 180
TitanFlex 48
titanium 16, 17, 22–23
Tommasini, Irio 22
tools 178–183
top tubes 12, 32, 34
Torx keys 178, 179
Trek
    aluminium frames 24–25
    BB90 bottom brackets 41, 103
    carbon-fibre frames 18–19
    Domane 48
    E2 steerer tapers 44
    Madone KVF 33, 39
TRP 141, 143
TTT 149, 153, 154

tubes 32–41
tubular rims 60
tubular tyres 64–65, 67, 181
TVT (Technique du Verre Tissé) 18, 40
tyres 12, 48, 49, 62–69, 66, 67, 180–181

U

UCI (Union Cycliste Internationale) 117, 149
Ullrich, Jan 24, 158
UnicaNitor 157
Union Cycliste Internationale (UCI) 117, 149
Universal 129
USE 150

V

V-Brake 140
valve stems 12
Van Nicholas 22
Vittoria 66, 109
Vitus 24, 42
Vuelta a España 18

W

weight 18
Weinmann 133
Welch, Charles 63
Westwood 60, 127, 186
wheel rims 54–55, 60–61
wheel tension 56–59
wheels 12, 51–81
Whippet, The 29, 48
Wiggins, Sir Bradley 96

Y

Young's modulus 16, 79, 186

Z

Zertz 49
Zipp 61, 150
Zuelle, Alex 22

Picture Credits

Cover, water bottle © Science in Sport (SiS) plc.

p. 4–5, 8–9, 31, 37, 69, 121 © www.giant-bicycles.com
p.10, 140, 172 photographs by Jean-Philippe Ehrmann
© LOOK Cycle
p. 29 © SSPL via Getty Images
p. 30 top © The Online Bicycle Museum / www.oldbike.eu
p. 30 bottom, 53 © Harlow Museum and Science Alive
p. 36, 150, 151 © Cinelli Archive
p. 39 © Trek Bicycle Corporation Ltd.
p. 45, 67, 135, 178–9 © Shutterstock
p. 47 © Michael Shields / Creative Commons
p. 54 © 2013 by Ghisallo Wooden Rims. Published by permission
of Antonio Cermenati / www.cerchiinlegnoghisallo.com
p. 61 © Trek Bicycle Corporation Ltd.
p. 64 © iStock photo
p. 66, 68 © Continental Tyres Ltd
p. 69 based on a diagram curtsey of Continental Tyres Ltd
p. 73 © Mavic
p. 85, 88, 95, 100 left, middle & bottom right, 103 top, 104, 119,
137, 145, 170, 176, 182 bottom © Shimano
p. 87 left © Speedplay, Inc.
p. 96 © OsymetricUSA
p. 100 © RaceFace / © FSA – Full Speed Ahead
p. 101 © Cannondale / cyclingsportsgroup.co.uk
p. 111 photograph by Ray Dobbins
p. 113 © SRAM
p. 118, 123 bottom, 144 © Sun Race Sturmey-Archer Inc.
p. 122, 175, 177 © Condor Cycles / www.condorcycles.com
p. 123 top © Miche
p. 131 © Nokon
p. 136 © Magura
p. 138 © Mafac
p. 149, 151 top, 157, 161 © Brooks
p. 168–169, 173 © Garmin
p. 171 photograph by Gary Geiger / © PowerTap
p. 181 © Rema Tip Top

Technical illustrations by Matt Pagett
All other images photographed by Neal Grundy

Acknowledgements

Thanks to Chris Garrison at Trek Bicycle Corporation,
Mark Reilly and Jim Walker at Enigma Bikes, Cliff Shrubb,
the late Ken Bird, Luke Evans and Max Glaskin and, most
of all, my wife Jan for her endless patience and encouragement